Women of the American Revolution

Titles in the Women in History series include:

Women of Ancient Rome
Women of the Civil War
Women of the Middle Ages
Women of the 1960s

WOMEN IN HISTORY

Women of the American Revolution

Louise Chipley Slavicek

LUCENT
BOOKS®

THOMSON

GALE

San Diego • Detroit • New York • San Francisco • Cleveland • New Haven, Conn. • Waterville, Maine • London • Munich

THOMSON

™

for James M. Slavicek

© 2003 by Lucent Books. Lucent Books is an imprint of The Gale Group, Inc.,
a division of Thomson Learning, Inc.

Lucent Books® and Thomson Learning™ are trademarks used herein under license.

For more information, contact
Lucent Books
27500 Drake Rd.
Farmington Hills, MI 48331-3535
Or you can visit our Internet site at http://www.gale.com

LIBRARY OF CONGRESS CATALOGING-IN-PUBLICATION DATA

Slavicek, Louise Chipley, 1956–
    Women of the American Revolution / by Louise Chipley Slavicek.
        v. cm. — (Women in history series)
Includes bibliographical references and index.
Contents: Introduction: America in the Revolutionary era — The prewar crisis:
American women resist — American women at war: aiding the patriot cause on
and off the battlefield — Women camp followers — Patriot women face new
challenges at home — Loyalist and pacifist women — Native American women —
African American women — Epilogue: American women after the Revolution.
    ISBN 1-59018-172-7 (hardback : alk. paper)
    1. United States—History—Revolution, 1775–1783—Women—Juvenile litera-
ture. 2. United States—History—Revolution, 1775–1783—Social aspects—Juvenile
literature. 3. Women—United States—History—18th century—Juvenile literature.
[1. Unites States—History—Revolution, 1775–1783—Women. 2. United States—
History—Revolution, 1775–1783—Social aspects. 3. Women—History—18th century.] I. Title. II Series.
    E276 .S57 2003
    973.3 '082—dc21

2002000456

Printed in the United States of America

Contents

Foreword 6

Introduction: America During the Revolutionary Era 8

Chapter 1:

American Women and Prewar Resistance 14

Chapter 2:

Patriot Women at War 27

Chapter 3:

Women Camp Followers 41

Chapter 4:

Patriot Women on the Home Front 55

Chapter 5:

Loyalist and Pacifist Women 68

Chapter 6:

Native American Women 81

Chapter 7:

African American Women 93

Epilogue:

American Women After the Revolutionary War 106

Notes 111

For Further Reading 117

Works Consulted 118

Index 122

Picture Credits 127

About the Author 128

Foreword

The story of the past as told in traditional historical writings all too often leaves the impression that if men are not the only actors in the narrative, they are assuredly the main characters. With a few notable exceptions, males were the political, military, and economic leaders in virtually every culture throughout recorded time. Since traditional historical scholarship focuses on the public arenas of government, foreign relations, and commerce, the actions and ideas of men—or at least of powerful men—are naturally at the center of conventional accounts of the past.

In the last several decades, however, many historians have abandoned their predecessors' emphasis on "great men" to explore the past "from the bottom up," a phenomenon that has had important consequences for the study of women's history. These social historians, as they are known, focus on the day-to-day experiences of the "silent majority"—those people typically omitted from conventional scholarship because they held relatively little political or economic sway within their societies. In the new social history, members of ethnic and racial minorities, factory workers, peasants, slaves, children, and women are no longer relegated to the background but are placed at the very heart of the narrative.

Around the same time social historians began broadening their research to include women and other previously neglected elements of society, the feminist movement of the late 1960s and 1970s was also bringing unprecedented attention to the female heritage. Feminists hoped that by examining women's past experiences, contemporary women could better understand why and how gender-based expectations had developed in their societies, as well as how they might reshape inherited—and typically restrictive—economic, social, and political roles in the future.

Today, some four decades after the feminist and social history movements gave new impetus to the study of women's history, there is a rich and continually growing body of work on all aspects of women's lives in the past. The Lucent Books Women in History series draws upon this abundant and diverse literature to introduce students to women's experiences within a variety of past cultures and time periods in terms of the distinct roles they filled. In their capacities as workers, activists, and artists, women exerted significant influence on important events whether they conformed to or broke from traditional roles. The women in History titles depict extraordinary women who managed to attain positions of influence in their male-dominated societies, including such celebrated heroines as the feisty medieval queen Eleanor of Aquitaine, the brilliant propagandist of the American Revolution Mercy Otis Warren, and the courageous African American activist of the Civil War era, Harriet Tubman. Included as well are the stories of the ordinary—and often overlooked—women of the past who also helped shape their societies in myriad ways—moral, intellectual, and economic—without straying far from customary gender roles: the housewives and mothers, school teachers and church volunteers, midwives and nurses and wartime camp followers.

In this series, readers will discover that many of these unsung women took more significant parts in the great political and social upheavals of their day than has often been recognized. In *Women of the American Revolution,* for example, students will learn how American housewives assumed a crucial role in helping the Patriots win the war against Britain. They accomplished this by planting and harvesting fields, producing and trading goods, and doing whatever else was necessary to maintain the family farm or business in the absence of their soldier husbands despite the heavy burden of housekeeping and child care duties they already bore. By their self-sacrificing actions, competence, and ingenuity, these anonymous heroines not only kept their families alive, but kept the economy of their struggling young nation going as well during eight long years of war.

Each volume in this series contains generous commentary from the works of respected contemporary scholars, but the Women in History series particularly emphasizes quotations from primary sources such as diaries, letters, and journals whenever possible to allow the women of the past to speak for themselves. These firsthand accounts not only help students to better understand the dimensions of women's daily spheres—the work they did, the organizations they belonged to, the physical hardships they faced—but also how they viewed themselves and their actions in the light of their society's expectations for their sex.

The distinguished American historian Mary Beard once wrote that women have always been a "force in history." It is hoped that the books in this series will help students to better appreciate the vital yet often little known ways in which women of the past have shaped their societies and cultures.

Introduction:
America During the Revolutionary Era

The Revolutionary War (1775–1783) lasted for eight long years, testing the resiliency and courage of all Americans, male and female alike. Although women were barred from holding political office and serving in the armed forces, the struggle for independence shaped their experiences and outlooks in meaningful ways. The revolutionary crisis and the social, political, and economic upheavals that accompanied it touched the lives of women throughout British America, whether young or old, rich or poor, white, black, or Native American. American women, in turn, influenced every phase of their country's fight for independence, both through their individual endeavors and through their participation in organized movements.

America Wins Its Independence

The revolutionary crisis that so profoundly affected American women began long before shots were ever fired between Patriot and royal forces, when Britain became embroiled in a costly war with France for control of Canada. Britain's hard-won victory in 1763 left the country on the brink of bankruptcy. To help pay off Britain's staggering war debt and the ongoing costs of defending the American frontier, the British Parliament turned to its thirteen American colonies.

The creation of new taxes was at the heart of Parliament's plan to raise money in its North American colonies. The first of these levies, the Stamp Act of 1765, taxed printed items of all types, including legal documents, newspapers, pamphlets, and even playing cards. Since they had previously paid taxes only to their local and colonial governments, many Americans deeply resented the stamp tax. A prominent group of colonists, including lawyers and newspaper editors, argued that because Americans lacked representation in Parliament and their own legislatures had never approved the tax, the Stamp Act was unfair and ought to be repealed. When the Patriots, as the act's opponents came to be known, organized large public demonstrations against the tax, Parliament reluctantly gave in, revoking the Stamp Act just one year after its passage.

Not about to abandon its plans for raising money in America, in 1767 Parliament adopted the Townshend duties on paper, tea, and other products imported by the colonists from Britain. Once again the colonists reacted angri-

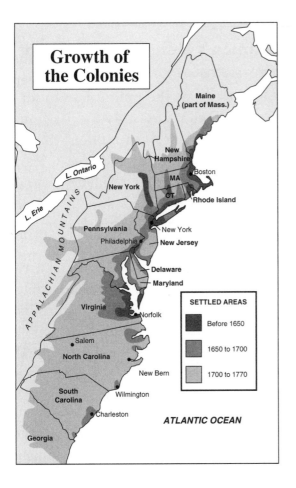

Growth of the Colonies

Maine (part of Mass.)

New Hampshire

L. Ontario

New York

MA

Boston

CT

Rhode Island

L. Erie

Pennsylvania

New York

Philadelphia

New Jersey

Delaware

Maryland

SETTLED AREAS

Virginia

Norfolk

Before 1650

1650 to 1700

Salem

1700 to 1770

North Carolina

New Bern

South Carolina

Wilmington

Charleston

ATLANTIC OCEAN

Georgia

APPALACHIAN MOUNTAINS

ly to the new revenue-raising act, and Britain was compelled to back down. After the Patriots organized a massive boycott of British goods, the royal government hesitantly withdrew all of the new duties, except the one on tea, which Parliament seemed to view as a token of its rightful authority over the colonists. For the Patriots, however, the tax on tea symbolized nothing less than British despotism. In 1773 Patriots thinly disguised as Native Americans dumped an entire shipload of English tea into Boston Harbor to protest the hated levy.

In the wake of the destructive Boston Tea Party, Parliament passed a series of repressive laws aimed at teaching the colonists a lesson. These Intolerable Acts, as the Patriots dubbed them, closed the port of Boston and stripped the Massachusetts legislature of most of its authority. Yet it soon became evident that the British had gravely overreached themselves in their frustration with the unruly colonists. Fearing a plot to deprive Americans of their political as well as their economic liberties, the other twelve colonies rallied behind Massachusetts, and the provincial Congress was convened to discuss a united response to British "tyranny." Before the Congress could reconvene, fighting erupted in April 1775 between civilian militia and British troops, popularly called Redcoats, searching for Patriot military stockpiles in Lexington and Concord, Massachusetts.

There would be no turning back now for the Patriots. Shortly after the battles at Lexington and Concord, Congress organized the Continental Army, and on July 4, 1776, the colonists formally declared their independence. Not every American favored independence, however. Historians estimate that perhaps two-fifths of the country's white population were active Patriots, and one-fifth were Loyalists or Tories, who supported the royal government. The remainder attempted to steer a middle course, including pacifists who opposed all warfare for religious reasons.

The months following the adoption of the Declaration of Independence were a trying time for the Patriots, who suffered a series of demoralizing defeats in the middle states. The following year brought the Americans renewed hope when their forces soundly defeated the British at the Battle of Saratoga in New York. In the wake of the impressive American victory, the French government decided to offer much-needed financial and military support to the Patriots.

Forced to reassess their strategy, the British shifted their focus from the northern to the southern states. Although the war in the South went badly for the Patriots at first, in October 1781 American-French forces decisively defeated the British at Yorktown, Virginia. Worn down by the long war, the British were finally ready to negotiate. In 1783 the Treaty of Paris officially ended the Revolutionary War, granting Americans independence and giving them title to all British land east of the Mississippi River, south of the Great Lakes, and north of Florida.

Women's Roles on the Eve of the Revolutionary Crisis

On the eve of the political and military crises that wracked America from 1765 to 1783, nearly 1 million women lived in the thirteen colonies. At least 90 percent of them resided in rural areas; the rest lived in towns or major cities such as Philadelphia, Boston, or New York City.

Whether they resided in the countryside or in the city, the lives of the white women who made up the majority of America's female population almost invariably revolved around home and hearth. As was true throughout the Western world, in the colonies a woman's proper place was believed to be within the domestic realm. Women were expected to dedicate their lives to running their

Colonial women were expected to work from dawn to dusk, devoted to housework and caring for their families.

households and caring for their families—no small undertaking in eighteenth-century America. The typical colonial woman toiled from dawn to dusk in the service of her household: preparing meals over blazing fires; sewing, washing, and ironing clothes; feeding poultry and milking cows; churning butter; and making soap and candles. In addition to her many housekeeping chores, she devoted much of her energy to caring for a seemingly endless procession of babies. As a rule,

colonial families were big: On the eve of the war, the average American woman had between five to eight children, giving birth every two or three years during her fertile years.

One consequence of the popular belief that a female's place was in the home serving her husband and children was the limited educational opportunities available to colonial women. Before the Revolution most girls received little if any formal schooling. Extensive intellectual

The Patriots emptied crates of tea into Boston Harbor to protest the hated tax levied by the British.

training was considered superfluous for girls whose adult lives were supposed to center on marriage, motherhood, and housekeeping.

In addition to restricted educational opportunities, most colonial women endured severely limited legal rights. Following British custom, married women could not own property; everything they inherited from their families and any wages they earned belonged to their husbands. Because they lacked property rights, married women could not engage in legal transactions such as selling or buying land or writing wills. Although unmarried women enjoyed the same property and legal rights as men, most colonial women chose to marry, for a single woman's position in eighteenth-century America was unenviable, to say the least. In a society that assumed that marriage and motherhood were a woman's central goals in life, single women were typically viewed as objects of pity and even contempt.

Whether married or single, American women were prohibited from voting and holding political office on the eve of the Revolution. As in the Old World, politics was a strictly male preserve in the thirteen colonies. Women were too busy with their domestic duties to think about political matters, it was believed, and furthermore lacked the intellectual training to make informed political decisions. Only males were encouraged to read and analyze the writings of the leading political thinkers of the past and present.

Although excluded from any formal role in political affairs, American women would nonetheless play a vital part in the colonies' long struggle with the Crown. In the process, they developed an unprecedented sense of political involvement and responsibility. This burgeoning political consciousness experienced by women from all regions and economic classes during the Revolutionary era had its roots in the turbulent decade between 1765 and 1775, when colonists took the road from resistance to all-out rebellion.

Chapter 1:
American Women and Prewar Resistance

In 1765, the year in which the Stamp Act was adopted, it was generally assumed in Britain and its colonies that politics fell well outside a woman's proper sphere. Since they were supposed to be completely absorbed in the private realm of home and family, women were expected to be uninterested in the public world of politics and government. Yet as the political struggle that would ultimately end in armed rebellion unfolded between 1765 and 1775, American women were inevitably caught up in the public debates of those momentous years. During the prewar period many women took a keen interest in political issues for the first time, as their private writings reveal. In time, political awareness would turn into political activism, as women became key participants in the carefully orchestrated boycotts of British goods that formed the heart of Patriot resistance to British "tyranny" before April 1775.

"Nothing Else Is Talked of": Growing Politically Aware

During the decade from the Stamp Act controversy to the battles of Lexington and Concord, American women's diaries and letters increasingly contained comments on political events and publications. Previously, their writings had focused almost exclusively on family news and other private concerns. Now many colonial women were exhibiting a deep appreciation of political affairs and ideas for the first time.

Indeed, American women could not have remained oblivious to the dramatic political events of the 1760s and early 1770s, even if they had wanted to. During the years preceding the Revolutionary War, the growing violence of mobs protesting unpopular parliamentary acts, the big public celebrations when hated laws were repealed, and the scores of political pamphlets and broadsides (posterlike notices) published throughout the colonies, all intruded upon the consciousness of women who had once been satisfied to leave politics to their male relations. As Sarah Franklin wrote from Philadelphia to her father, Benjamin Franklin, during the height of the Stamp Act controversy, politics was not merely the most interesting topic of conversation in town; it was the only one. "Nothing else is talked of,"[1] she observed.

During the escalating controversies of the prewar years, many women moved beyond simply reporting political happenings to expressing opinions

Women were drawn into the political debates of the time by unfair British edicts, such as this one banning all linen and woolen goods from Boston.

about them in their private writings. Since they had been taught from childhood that political discussion, like voting and other forms of direct political participation, was for men only, many American women felt uncomfortable stating their political views. Time after time, the age-old boundary between what was assumed to be the private feminine sphere and the public male sphere led women to apologize for their boldness even as they admitted the difficulty of keeping their political opinions to themselves. In 1767, for example, Anne Hooper of North Carolina felt compelled to justify her fascination with public events to a correspondent, explaining that she only discussed politics in her letters because "its being so much talked of here."[2] A year later Charity Clarke, a New York City teenager, fretted in a letter to a male cousin that the strong political opinions she had expressed in a previous letter would change "the Idea you would have of female softness in me."[3] Politics, she admitted, made her uneasy, for it was a subject she considered beyond her proper sphere. Like Hooper, Clarke felt obliged to defend her interest in political issues. Struggling to find the right words to justify her staunch Patriot views to her cousin, Clarke ended up simply declaring, "I cannot help them."[4]

Boycotting British Goods: Growing Activism

Although colonial women worried that men viewed political discussion as out of their province, as the prewar crisis escalated, women found themselves being recruited by Patriot leaders to participate in political activities, albeit in a fashion that meshed well with their traditional domestic role. During the late 1760s and early 1770s, Patriot spokesmen repeatedly called on American women to take part in consumer boycotts of English goods, the most potent weapon in the colonists' political arsenal before the Revolutionary War. By the mid-eighteenth century, the thirteen colonies had become a vital market for British imports such as tea, cloth,

Patriot women sign a petition agreeing not to drink tea during the tea boycott.

Persuading Women to Take Action

At first, some male Patriot leaders worried that it might prove difficult to persuade women to participate in the colonial boycotts. In 1769 South Carolina legislator Christopher Gadsden spoke bluntly to his male compatriots regarding how they might best convince their wives to cooperate with the boycotts. As Linda K. Kerber notes in *Women of the Republic,* Gadsden assumed that appealing to the women's "natural" desire to protect their children and homes above all else would be the most effective way to ensure their assistance.

I come here to the last, and what many say and think is the *greatest difficulty* of all we have to encounter, that is, to persuade our wives to give us their assistance. . . . Only let their husbands point out the necessity of such conduct; convince them, that it is the only thing that can save them and their children, from distress, slavery, and disgrace; their affections will be awakened, and cooperate with their reason. When that is done, all that is necessary will be done; for I am persuaded, that they will be then as anxious and persevering in this matter, as any the most zealous of us can possibly wish.

and paint. Consequently, Patriot leaders found nonimportation agreements, in which merchants pledged not to import British goods, and consumer boycotts, in which ordinary citizens spurned British products, highly effective means of protesting royal taxes.

Women, the Patriots' male leadership realized, were essential allies in the economic campaign they were conducting against Britain. As household managers, they possessed the power to make or break a boycott. Without the cooperation of American housewives, the Patriot legislator and spokesman Christopher Gadsden publicly conceded in 1769, "'tis impossible to succeed."[5]

And cooperate they did. Women's determination to support the Patriot cause through what they did or did not buy or consume was evident in all parts of the colonies. Women's commitment to the tea boycott of the late 1760s and early 1770s was particularly strong, despite the enormous popularity of tea drinking among female colonists. During the boycott some women forsook their beloved tea for coffee while countless others brewed homemade "liberty teas." Women across America exchanged recipes for these tea substitutes, which were concocted from a variety of native plants, including sage, strawberry, and raspberry. In Boston hundreds of Patriot housewives pledged not to drink tea except in cases of serious illness, and in Wilmington, North Carolina, townswomen burned their tea in a dramatic communal ceremony. Even young girls participated in the tea boycott. On a visit to the home of the royal governor of New Jersey, nine-year-old Susan Boudinot politely accepted a cup of tea, then shocked her host by defiantly tossing the cup's contents out of the drawing room window.

The Politics of Spinning

When Patriot leaders turned to consumer boycotts to force Britain to repeal new revenue-raising acts, the traditional female task of buying household items took on deep political significance. During the decade of protest that led to the Revolutionary War, another traditional female chore also became imbued with political symbolism: the making of cloth.

By the mid-eighteenth century, Americans were importing a great deal of cloth from Britain. Producing cloth at home involved many monotonous and time-consuming tasks, including spinning thread from wool or flax at a

A historical interpreter spins thread to make homespun, much as colonial women did during the Revolution.

wheel and weaving those threads into fabric on a loom. Because the chores of spinning and weaving were so labor-intensive, many busy American housewives preferred to buy at least some of their cloth ready-made from England. Typically, only poorer families or those who lived on remote farms produced all of their own clothing at home on the eve of the Revolutionary crisis.

After the consumer boycotts of the 1760s and early 1770s effectively cut off

British imports to the colonies, Patriot leaders called on American women to increase their production of homemade cloth, or homespun. By doing so, the Patriot spokesmen asserted, women could help the colonies replace their dependency on English imports with economic self-sufficiency. Demonstrating their deep commitment to the Patriot cause, thousands of American women responded to their leaders' call, embracing the tedious chores of spinning and weaving with newfound enthusiasm.

As home cloth production became politicized during the pre-Revolutionary era, female spinners and weavers proudly portrayed themselves in their diaries and letters as "a fighting army of amazones" (a reference to the race of warlike women described by the ancient Greeks) or reported that they felt "Nationaly"[6] as they toiled away at their wheels and looms. Since most American females learned to spin by the time they were eight years old, girls as well as adult women were caught up in the revolutionary fervor surrounding homespun. In Massachusetts eleven-year-old Anna Winslow recorded her personal contribution to the Patriot effort in her diary, asserting, "As I am (as we say) a daughter of liberty, I chuse to war [wear] as much of our own manufactory as pocible."[7]

Patriotic women and girls did not only produce homespun within the privacy of their own homes. Many also participated in communal displays of spinning. These spinning meetings, writes historian Joan R. Gundersen, became important "public rituals demonstrating colonial self-sufficiency and firmness"[8] as boycotts of British cloth and other imported goods emerged as the colonists' most powerful form of resistance to royal

Daughters of Liberty

Many of the women who participated in the colonial tea boycott referred to themselves as "Daughters of Liberty," after the male protest groups called "Sons of Liberty" that sprang up in America during the Stamp Act crisis. Although some Daughters of Liberty formed themselves into loosely knit groups, the name did not necessarily imply membership in a particular organization. Indeed, throughout the prewar period *Daughters of Liberty* was a more or less generic term that included any American women who took a stand against British policies.

taxation. In towns and cities across the colonies, groups of females, often referring to themselves as Daughters of Liberty, met to spin thread together, hoping by their actions both to demonstrate their own support for the Patriot cause and to encourage other women to follow their example.

Typically, spinning bees were held in the home of the local minister, the most prominent man in town. The gatherings attracted as many as one hundred participants, with spinners from all social and economic backgrounds, including the community's wealthiest families. The fact that even well-to-do women who could hire others to do their spinning attended bees lent an air of added respectability to the meetings, as an editorial in the *South Carolina Gazette* reveals. The participation of ladies from the colony's "best" families, the editorial proclaimed, clearly demonstrated it was not "a disgrace for one of our fair sex to be catched at a spinning bee."[9]

Wealthy or poor, most spinning bee participants were young, unmarried women. Married women were generally too engrossed in their domestic responsibilities to attend the day-long affairs. Nonetheless, there were notable exceptions. In an article published in the *New Hampshire Gazette* in 1769, for instance, a minister described a large spinning meeting held at his home in Brookfield.

Among the women who attended, the pastor noted with obvious admiration, was one tireless matron "who did the morning work of a large family, made her cheese, etc. and then rode more than two miles, and carried her own wheel, and sat down to spin at nine in the morning, and by seven in the evening spun 53 knots, and went home to milking."[10]

The meeting at the New Hampshire minister's home, like bees held throughout the American colonies during the late 1760s and early 1770s, probably followed a set pattern. Between twenty and fifty women, all dressed in homespun and hauling their own wheels, would arrive at their minister's house around dawn, remaining there until dusk. Refreshments, usually provided by community members, featured native herbal teas and produce. Before departing, the spinners would present their output to the minister, who used the thread for his own household or donated it to charity. Many of the gatherings concluded with the performance of an original poem or song praising the sacrifices made by Patriot women and emphasizing their importance to the struggle for liberty. The following song honoring the contributions of female Patriots was performed at a bee held in Bridgewater, Connecticut, in 1769 and later published in a local newspaper:

Women of the American Revolution

Foreign productions she rejects

With nobleness of Mind,

For Home commodities, to which

She's prudently inclin'd . . .

She Cloaths herself and family,

And all the Sons of need;

Were all thus virtuous, soon we'd find,

Our Land from Slav'ry free'd.[11]

Like the laudatory song performed at the Bridgewater bee, the published accounts of spinning bees that appeared frequently in newspapers during the prewar years stressed the participants' critical contribution to the American cause. For example, an editorial in the *Boston Evening Post* celebrated the vital political assistance offered by female spinners, asserting that "the industry and frugality of American ladies must exalt their character in the Eyes of the World and serve to show how greatly they are contributing to bring about the political salvation of a whole Continent."[12]

Many women were obviously proud of the public respect and attention they received for taking part in spinning bees and consumer boycotts. Thus, when a Boston satirist dared to mock female Patriots in a newspaper piece, hinting that they scorned political discussion at their spinning meetings in favor of "such trifling subjects as Dress, Scandal and Detraction," Boston's women were filled

Women and Patriot Crowds

T he streets of America's cities were an important arena for protest during the prewar years. From the Stamp Act crisis on, mass demonstrations helped gain attention for the Patriot cause. Although Patriot crowds were primarily composed of working-class men, they typically included some working-class women as well, particularly shopkeepers and street vendors. Women were especially prominent in the public funeral processions held for protesters killed by Redcoats, and they also participated in the tarring and feathering of merchants who shunned nonimportation agreements, the hangings of tax collectors in effigy, and the big public celebrations held in many cities following repeal of controversial parliamentary acts.

Women in southern plantation houses like this one were expected to confine their activities to household concerns. They pushed the boundaries of appropriate female behavior by writing and signing public petitions.

with righteous indignation. In a letter to the editor, a group of townswomen attacked the demeaning article, declaring it had "scandalously insulted" their sex. "Inferior in abusive sarcasm, in personal invective, in low wit, we glory to be, but inferior in veracity, sincerity, love of virtue, of liberty and of our country, we would not willingly be to any,"[13] the women proudly asserted.

The Edenton Petition

Patriotic women who declined to purchase British products, made their own thread and cloth, or brewed their own herbal teas were participating in political acts in the course of carrying out traditional women's tasks. During the course of the prewar crises, however, some American women became politically active in ways that challenged the limits of what their society perceived as acceptable female conduct.

One way in which Patriot women pushed the boundaries of what was considered appropriate female behavior was in the writing and signing of public petitions. The most famous political petition created and signed by women during the prewar years was the Edenton Petition, which was endorsed by fifty-one women in Edenton, North Carolina, in 1774 and was published in a provincial newspaper. The petition stated the women's determination to support a recent colonial resolution boycotting British goods, asserting that American women had not only a right but also an obligation to take a political stand in the dispute between their country and the royal government:

> As we cannot be indifferent on any occasion that appears nearly to affect the peace and happiness of our country, and as it has been thought necessary for the public good, to enter into several particular resolves by a meeting of members deputed from the whole Province, it is a duty which we owe, not only to our near and dear relations and connections . . . but to ourselves, who are essentially interested in their welfare, to do everything as far as lies in our power, to testify our sincere adherence to the same; and we do therefore accordingly subscribe this paper, as a witness of our fixed intention and solemn determination to do so.[14]

During the nineteenth century collective statements like the Edenton Petition would become highly effective political devices for American women seeking greater rights. During the 1770s, however, the idea of a public political manifesto authored and endorsed by women was startlingly novel to Americans and Europeans alike. The fact that it was almost unheard-of for women to make formal political statements opened the Edenton petitioners to the ridicule of their political enemies. A widely circulated British political cartoon entitled the

Mercy Otis Warren anonymously published some of the most effective propaganda of the prewar era.

"Edenton Ladies Tea Party" poked bitter fun at the Edenton women, portraying them as aggressive, sluttish, and unattractive. Other British and Loyalist critics snidely suggested that the Edenton Petition and the colonial boycott movement it endorsed had inaugurated a sexual revolution in America, creating mannish females and emasculated males.

Mercy Otis Warren: Patriot Propagandist

If an eighteenth-century woman was stepping out of her usual realm to publicly endorse a political petition, she had to venture even farther out of her "proper" sphere to create political propaganda. One of the few American females who dared to enter the male preserve of political propaganda during the prewar era was Mercy Otis Warren.

It was perhaps inevitable that Warren should become interested in politics. The sister of one leading Patriot, James Otis, and the wife of another, the Massachusetts legislator James Warren, Mercy Otis Warren spent all of her adult life in fiercely political circles. As knowledgeable about literature and history as she was

Loyalist Women and Prewar Political Controversy

Patriot women did not hold a monopoly on political consciousness or activism during the prewar years. Some female supporters of the royal government also took political stands during that turbulent period. For instance, some female Loyalists made a point of serving imported tea when they entertained friends and neighbors. More daringly, a few female shopkeepers demonstrated their support for British policies by refusing to honor colonial nonimportation agreements. In 1768, for example, sisters Anne and Betsy Cummings of Boston continued to sell British goods in their shop in defiance of the local Patriot committee's orders. When committee members confronted Betsy in her store one day, she refused to back down, scolding the men for attempting to "inger [injure] two industrious Girls who ware Striving in an honest way to Git their Bread," notes Mary Beth Norton in *Liberty's Daughters: The Revolutionary Experience of American Women.*

about politics, Warren was remarkably well educated for a woman of her time. Although she received little formal schooling, as a girl Warren was permitted to sit in on her brothers' tutoring sessions. Early on she showed an aptitude for writing, particularly for poetry and drama.

During the early 1770s, as the political crisis between Great Britain and its colonies escalated, Warren decided to put her natural talent for writing to work for the Patriots. Although her male relations encouraged her efforts, Warren realized that others outside her family might censure her for presuming to meddle in the traditionally male world of political propaganda. Consequently, she published her political writings anonymously, including the drama *The Adulateur* (1772), a biting satire of Massachusetts's royal governor, and two other plays lampooning British rule and supporters in America, *The Defeat* (1773) and *The Group* (1775). Considered by some historians as among the most effective propaganda of the prewar era, Warren's dramas were reprinted in newspapers throughout the colonies. The fact that the plays were published in newspapers may seem unusual; but like many dramas of the time, Warren's works were designed to be read, not performed by actors.

Despite the popularity of her plays, Warren was wracked by doubts regarding the propriety of a woman writing scathing political satires. In a letter to her friend John Adams in 1775, she wondered if the "personal Acrimony" (harshness) she expressed in her plays toward royal officials was offensive to the small circle of male relatives and friends who realized she was the author; did they secretly view her as "deficient"[15] in feminine qualities? Adams assured Warren that it was entirely appropriate for her to use her considerable natural talent for satire to bolster the Patriot cause. Yet Adams's supportive words apparently did little to ease Warren's doubts, for a year later she suspected him of asking for her political opinions for the sole purpose of mocking her and her entire sex:

Your asking my opinion on so momentous a point as the form of government which ought to be preferred by a people about to shake off the fetters of monarchic . . . tyranny may be designed to ridicule the sex for paying any attention to political matters. Yet I shall venture to give you a serious reply. Notwithstanding the love of dress, dancing, and equipage, notwithstanding the fondness for finery, folly and fashion, is so strongly predominant in the female mind, I hope never to see a Monarchy established in America.[16]

During the decade of protest that preceded the Revolutionary War, American women became politically aware and active to an extent previously unknown in the colonies or the mother country. Few went so far as to publish political propaganda, as did Mercy Otis Warren, or to create formal political petitions, as did the women of Edenton. Yet countless colonial women demonstrated their involvement in the political controversies of the day by discussing public events in their private writings, participating in boycotts of British goods, and producing homespun to help end American dependence on imported cloth. During the eight-year-long military conflict that began with the battles at Lexington and Concord in April 1775, women would become even more deeply involved in the traditionally male world of public affairs. And as they aided the Patriot cause on and off the battlefield, American women would express their patriotism in a variety of unprecedented and influential ways.

Chapter 2:
Patriot Women at War

D uring the Revolutionary War American women boldly assumed a variety of duties customarily assigned to men in their desire to aid the Patriot cause. In a home front war, the services of women as fund-raisers, spies, messengers, saboteurs, and even as fighters was vital, even though none of these roles had traditionally been viewed by colonial or European society as appropriate for females.

Women Fund-Raisers

From the very beginning of the war, American women provided material support to the Patriot effort. Women all over the country gathered scrap metal from candlesticks, kettles, and pewter plates to be melted down for bullets and cannonballs. The individual endeavors of countless women made a real difference, for the young American government had few resources with which to equip its armed forces.

As the war dragged on and both provisions and morale were in increasingly short supply among the Patriot forces, some women organized their efforts for the soldiers on a far larger and more public scale than ever before. In the summer of 1780, in the wake of a series of devastating Patriot losses in the South, a group of Philadelphia women created the first national women's organization in American history to raise money for the hard-pressed troops. In this unprecedented project, the women built on the feeling of political involvement that had spurred them to organize spinning bees and participate in boycotts during the prewar years.

The women's campaign to aid the troops was launched with the publication of a broadside written by Esther de Berdt Reed, the wife of the governor of Pennsylvania. Entitled *Sentiments of an American Woman,* it called on Patriot women to economize, donating the money they saved to the demoralized and ragged soldiers. *Sentiments of an American Woman* offered a new vision of female patriotism by boldly declaring the natural inclination of American women to be active patriots. Like their male compatriots, American females were "born for liberty, disdaining the irons of tyrannic Government,"[17] Reed proclaimed. And "if opinions and manners" forbade them "to march to glory by the same paths as the Men," she noted regarding the barring of her sex from formal military service, American women were nonetheless as devoted to "the public good"[18] as their husbands or brothers.

Despite her belief in the ability and tendency of American women to be forceful, committed patriots, Reed felt compelled to address the issue of propriety in her broadside. Some men, she realized, might disapprove of her scheme to involve women in fund-raising, customarily considered a male task. Yet any American who was a "good citizen," Reed maintained, could only "applaud our efforts for the relief of the armies which defend our lives, our possessions, our liberty."[19] By thus implying that anyone critical of the scheme would be "unpatriotic," notes historian Mary Beth Norton, Reed "cleverly defused possible traditionalist objections even before they could be advanced."[20]

Reed's call to patriotism drew an immediate response from the women of her hometown. An organization known as the Association was formed, and commit-

Esther de Berdt Reed boldly declared in her broadside that women could be devoted and active patriots.

THE SENTIMENTS of an **AMERICAN WOMAN.**

ON the commencement of actual war, the Women of America manifested a firm resolution to contribute as much as could depend on them, to the deliverance of their country. Animated by the purest patriotism, they are sensible of sorrow at this day, in not offering more than barren wishes for the success of so glorious a Revolution. They aspire to render themselves more really useful; and this sentiment is universal from the north to the south of the Thirteen United States. Our ambition is kindled by the fame of those heroines of antiquity, who have rendered their sex illustrious, and have proved to the universe, that, if the weakness of our Constitution, if opinion and manners did not forbid us to march to glory by the same paths as the Men, we should at least equal, and sometimes surpass them in our love for the public good. I glory in all that which my sex has done great and commendable. I call to mind with enthusiasm and with admiration, all those acts of courage, of constancy and patriotism, which history has transmitted to us: The people favoured by Heaven, preserved from destruction by the virtues, the zeal and the resolution of Deborah, of Judith, of Esther! The fortitude of the mother of the Macchabees, in giving up her sons to die before her eyes: Rome saved from the fury of a victorious enemy by the efforts of Volumnia, and other Roman Ladies: So many famous sieges where the Women have been seen forgetting the weakness of their sex, building new walls, digging trenches with their feeble hands; furnishing arms to their defenders, they themselves darting the missile weapons on the enemy, resigning the ornaments of their apparel, and their fortune, to fill the public treasury, and to hasten the deliverance of their country; burying themselves under its ruins; throwing themselves into the flames rather than submit to the disgrace of humiliation before a proud enemy.

Born for liberty, disdaining to bear the irons of a tyrannic Government, we associate ourselves to the grandeur of those Sovereigns, cherished and revered, who have held with so much splendour the scepter of the greatest States, The Batildas, the Elizabeths, the Maries, the Catharines, who have extended the empire of liberty, and contented to reign by sweetness and justice, have broken the chains of slavery, forged by tyrants in the times of ignorance and barbarity. The Spanish Women, do they not make, at this moment, the most patriotic sacrifices, to encrease the means of victory in the hands of their Sovereign. He is a friend to the French Nation. They are our allies. We call to mind, doubly interested, that it was a French Maid who kindled up amongst her fellow-citizens, the flame of patriotism buried under long misfortunes: It was the Maid of Orleans who drove from the kingdom of France the ancestors of those same British, whose odious yoke we have just shaken off; and whom it is necessary that we drive from this Continent.

But I must limit myself to the recollection of this small number of atchievements. Who knows if persons disposed to censure, and sometimes too severely with regard to us, may not disapprove our appearing acquainted even with the actions of which our sex boasts? We are at least certain, that he cannot be a good citizen who will not applaud our efforts for the relief of the armies which defend our lives, our possessions, our liberty? The situation of our soldiery has been represented to me; the evils inseparable from war, and the firm and generous spirit which has enabled them to support these. But it has been said, that they may apprehend, that, in the course of a long war, the view of their distresses may be lost, and their services be forgotten. Forgotten! never; I can answer in the name of all my sex. Brave Americans, your disinterestedness, your courage, and your constancy will always be dear to America, as long as she shall preserve her virtue.

We know that at a distance from the theatre of war, if we enjoy any tranquility, it is the fruit of your watchings, your labours, your dangers. If I live happy in the midst of my family; if my husband cultivates his field, and reaps his harvest in peace; if, surrounded with my children, I myself nourish the youngest, and press it to my bosom, without being afraid of seeing myself separated from it, by a ferocious enemy; if the house in which we dwell; if our barns, our orchards are safe at the present time from the hands of those incendiaries, it is to you that we owe it. And shall we hesitate to evidence to you our gratitude? Shall we hesitate to wear a cloathing more simple; hair dressed less elegant, while at the price of this small privation, we shall deserve your benedictions. Who, amongst us, will not renounce with the highest pleasure, those vain ornaments, when she shall consider that the valiant defenders of America will be able to draw some advantage from the money which she may have laid out in these; that they will be better defended from the rigours of the seasons, that after their painful toils, they will receive some extraordinary and unexpected relief; that these presents will perhaps be valued by them at a greater price, when they will have it in their power to say: *This is the offering of the Ladies.* The time is arrived to display the same sentiments which animated us at the beginning of the Revolution, when we renounced the use of teas, however agreeable to our taste, rather than receive them from our persecutors; when we made it appear to them that we placed former necessaries in the rank of superfluities, when our liberty was interested; when our republican and laborious hands spun the flax, prepared the linen intended for the use of our soldiers; when exiles and fugitives we supported with courage all the evils which are the concomitants of war, let us not lose a moment; let us be engaged to offer the homage of our gratitude at the altar of military valour, and you, our brave deliverers, while mercenary slaves combat to cause you to share with them, the irons with which they are loaded, receive with a free hand our offering, the purest which can be presented to your virtue,

BY AN **AMERICAN WOMAN.**

Women of the American Revolution

Aiding the Soldiers at Valley Forge

In addition to the organized efforts of the women of the Association to aid the Continental soldiers, individual women made great sacrifices to provide material assistance to the troops. One of the most energetic and committed of these was Mary Frazier. During the eighteenth century, armies usually campaigned during the warmer months, then settled into winter quarters during the coldest part of the year. Frazier, who lived near the Continental Army's winter camp at Valley Forge, Pennsylvania, sought to help the suffering Continentals during the bitterly cold months they endured there in late 1777 and early 1778. Warm clothing and blankets as well as food were in critically short supply at Valley Forge, and Frazier was determined to do something for the shivering and sickly troops. According to a contemporary account reprinted in Linda K. Kerber's *Women of the Republic,* Frazier rode

day after day collecting from neighbors and friends far and near, whatever they could spare for the comfort of the destitute soldiers, the blankets, and yarn, and half worn clothing thus obtained she brought to her own house, where they would be patched, and darned, and made wearable and comfortable, the stockings newly footed, or new ones knit, adding what clothing she could give of her own. She often sat up half the night, sometimes all, to get clothing ready. Then with it, and whatever could be obtained for food, she would have packed on her horse and set out on the cold lonely journey to the camp—which she went to repeatedly during the winter.

tees of women were assigned to canvass each neighborhood in the city. Although soliciting money from strangers was considered unconventional behavior for a respectable woman at the time, women from Philadelphia's most distinguished families eagerly volunteered to help. "I am . . . Honoured with this business,"[21] the wealthy matron Mary Morris wrote proudly to a friend regarding her role as a canvasser.

Morris had reason to be proud. The Association's door-to-door campaign was remarkably successful, raising three hundred thousand dollars in paper money (seventy-five hundred dollars in gold) from sixteen hundred contributors. All classes of Philadelphia's female

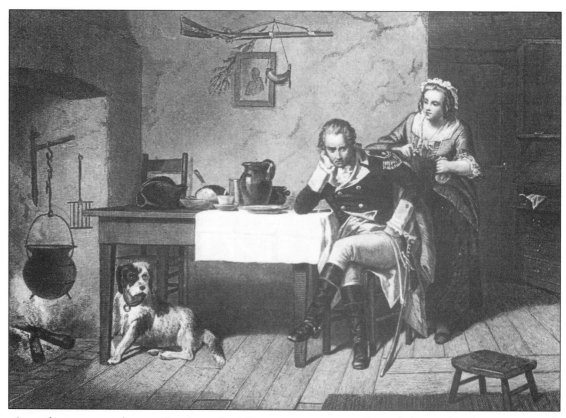

A southern woman begs a Continental soldier to accept money. General George Washington rejected cash contributions from patriotic women in favor of hand-sewn shirts for soldiers.

society joined in the effort, from the free African American who donated "seven shillings sixpence" and whose name was recorded by the canvassers as simply "Phyllis,"[22] to the aristocratic Countess de Luzerne, who contributed six thousand dollars in paper money.

Even more impressive than the amount of money collected was that the Association carried out its fund-raising scheme without male guidance, despite the popular assumption that females pos-

sessed inferior financial and organizational skills. Since they had raised the money without male direction, the women naturally assumed that they had the right to spend it as they saw fit, too. Reed wrote to George Washington, then commander in chief of the Continental Army, with the Association's decision; the women wanted to give each soldier a small gift of cash "to be entirely at his own disposal."[23] Fearing that too many soldiers would squander the cash on alcohol instead of using it for necessary supplies, however, Washington firmly declined Reed's offer. In the end, it was agreed that the women would use the money to make shirts for the soldiers, each one labeled with the name of the woman who had sewn it. By late 1780 Association members had stitched more than two thousand shirts for the troops. Ironically, notes Norton, the women, who had "embarked on a very unfeminine enterprise" when they became involved in large-scale fund-raising, were ultimately diverted into a "traditional domestic role"[24] by Washington, that of seamstress.

Although Washington prevailed in the matter of cash donations to the soldiers, the women of Philadelphia had nonetheless accomplished something unprecedented: They had sparked the creation of a nationwide organization conceived and directed entirely by women. From the start, Reed had encouraged women throughout America to participate in the fund-raising, with local governors' wives coordinating efforts. In New Jersey, Maryland, Delaware, and Virginia, their hopes were realized when women organized themselves into committees to collect money for the troops. The tens of thousands of dollars they raised were used for purchasing much-needed clothing for the soldiers. "Although it is impossible to estimate how many women may have worked with the Association," writes historian Linda Grant De Pauw, "it was unquestionably the largest organization of American women up to that time and for at least half a century afterward."[25]

Women Messengers

During the course of the Revolution, some American women dared to venture even farther from the customary female sphere in support of their country than did the ladies of the Association, risking their lives as messengers for the Patriot forces. Paul Revere may be the most famous messenger of the war, but Patriot women also served as couriers, with some carrying out missions every bit as dangerous as Revere's midnight gallop through the Massachusetts countryside in April 1775.

Two of the boldest female messengers of the Revolutionary War were teenagers. The first, sixteen-year-old Sybil Ludington, was the daughter of a Patriot militia commander in Patterson, New York. One spring night in 1777, an exhausted rider arrived at the Ludington farm with the news that British troops were raiding a Continental supply base in nearby Danbury, Connecticut. Someone had to bring the message to Ludington's unit to turn out immediately. Like other Patriot militia units,

Elizabeth Burgin and
the American POWs

During the course of the Revolutionary War, more American soldiers died as prisoners of war than perished on the battlefield. British prisons were notorious for their terrible conditions, and none were worse than the prison ships of New York City. On these floating prisons, food, blankets, and other critical supplies were scarce, and deadly diseases spread like wildfire through the cramped and poorly ventilated quarters. One New Yorker who was determined to try to help the prisoners was a widow and mother named Elizabeth Burgin. Burgin visited the floating prisons as frequently as she could, bringing the men baskets of food and other supplies. Since women were the only Americans permitted to visit the prison ships, in 1779 a Patriot officer sought Burgin's assistance in carrying out a daring escape scheme. Over a period of weeks, Burgin helped more than two hundred prisoners escape from the ship by quietly alerting them to the officer's plan. When the British became aware of the plot and Burgin's role in it, they offered a reward of two hundred pounds for her capture—a large sum at the time. Burgin hid in New York City for two weeks before escaping to Patriot lines. In 1780 Congress awarded her a pension for her services to the Patriot effort.

Ludington's soldiers lived at home, on widely scattered farms, and not in barracks. Sybil, an expert rider, volunteered to sound the alarm. She rode for nearly forty miles that rainy, moonless night, rousing her father's men by banging on their doors with a stick as she galloped past. It was too late to save the supply base, but Ludington's unit helped the Continentals drive the Redcoats out of Connecticut and all the way back to New York City.

Like Sybil Ludington, Emily Geiger of South Carolina was just sixteen years old when she volunteered to serve as a messenger for the Patriots. In the summer of 1781, the commander of the Continental Army in the South, General Nathanael Greene, was camped near Geiger's house. Faced by an advancing British force much bigger than his own, he urgently needed reinforcements from the closest Patriot unit, that of Thomas Sumter, nearly one hundred miles away.

A messenger was required, someone who was both resourceful and courageous, for the countryside swarmed with British and Loyalist soldiers. Convinced that a girl could pass where a man or boy could not, Emily bravely volunteered for the mission. As a precaution, she memorized Greene's message before concealing it in her clothes. On the second day of her journey, British soldiers stopped Emily and escorted her to their camp. Since the rules of modesty forbade them from searching a female, Geiger's gentlemanly captors went off to find a woman to conduct the search for them. While they were gone, Geiger ripped Greene's message into small pieces and swallowed it. When the woman assigned to search Emily found nothing, the Redcoats apologized to the teenager and sent her on her way. The following day, Geiger arrived at Sumter's camp and conveyed Greene's message to the general.

Women Spies

Since femininity was popularly associated with traits such as delicacy and timidity, women messengers found an excellent cover for their activities in their society's gender-rooted assumptions. As spies for the Patriot cause, American women also used their femininity as a guise to collect critical military intelligence.

One of the most effective female spies of the Revolution was Lydia Darragh. During the British occupation of Philadelphia in 1777, Darragh, a midwife and undertaker, lived across the street from the tavern where the British made their headquarters. In need of more space, British officers commandeered Darragh's dining room for their war councils. One day Darragh overheard them plotting a surprise attack on the Continental camp at nearby Whitemarsh, Pennsylvania. Darragh knew that she had to get through to the Patriot forces, and quickly. The next morning, using the excuse that she needed to visit a mill near Whitemarsh, she received permission to pass through British lines. Darragh promptly sneaked off to the American camp to alert Washington. When the British attack came, the general's army was ready, and the Redcoats were forced to withdraw to Philadelphia. Incredibly, when the infuriated British officers began hunting for the spy in their midst, they never seriously considered Darragh as a suspect. Apparently it did not occur to them that a woman might possess the necessary courage or cunning to be a spy.

Six months after the failed British attack on Whitemarsh, the royal army evacuated Philadelphia. British attention now turned from the North to the South, where another female Patriot would take advantage of her era's gender stereotypes to spy for her side. On the South Carolina frontier, fifteen-year-old Laodicea "Dicey" Langston outwitted Loyalist troops stationed near her family's farm for months, evidently because they failed to imagine that a sweet-faced girl could also be a secret agent. As she went about her chores, Dicey furtively observed the Loyalists' every move, relaying any interesting information to Patriot militia units in the neighboring county. One night she traveled alone for 20 miles through the dark countryside to warn her brother and his detachment of a planned Loyalist attack. The next day, after finding the Patriot camp empty, the Loyalist troops finally came to the realization that Dicey had been spying on them. According to some accounts, the enraged soldiers threatened to kill Dicey's father in revenge, but they backed off when Dicey threw herself in

Catherine Schuyler sets fire to her family's wheatfields to prevent the British from confiscating them.

Women of the American Revolution

The Militiawomen of Groton, Massachusetts

❧

During the battles of Lexington and Concord in April 1775, the militiamen of nearby Groton, Massachusetts, rode off to join the fighting. Fearing that Redcoats might try to sneak into Groton while the militiamen were away, about thirty townswomen under the direction of Prudence Wright and Sarah Shattuck set off to guard Jewett Bridge, which anyone entering town would have to cross. Armed with pitchforks, the women hid in the bushes until they saw a man on horseback approaching the bridge. They ambushed and searched the rider, who turned out to be a Loyalist carrying a secret dispatch to British headquarters in Boston. Wright, Shattuck, and their impromptu band of "militiawomen" promptly arrested the Loyalist messenger, then handed him and his dispatch over to the local Patriot Committee of Safety. Many years later a granite monument was erected near Jewett Bridge to commemorate the women's bravery that April night.

front of her parent, declaring that they would have to shoot her first.

Women Saboteurs

In addition to serving as messengers and spies, Patriot women also assumed another traditionally masculine role during the Revolutionary War, that of saboteur. In 1780 South Carolinian Martha Bratton, left alone by her husband to guard a warehouse full of gunpowder, got wind of a British plot to steal the ammunition. Before the Redcoats could get their hands on the scarce commodity, Bratton set fire to the gunpowder, destroying every bit of it.

Other women saboteurs set fire to their own property to keep it from falling into enemy hands. In 1781 Rebecca Motte, a widow from Charleston, South Carolina, helped Patriot troops set fire to her own home to smoke out the British troops using her hillside residence as a fort. A few years earlier, in upstate New York, Catherine Schuyler set fire to her family's extensive wheat crop to prevent the British troops advancing on nearby Saratoga from confiscating it. When the British arrived at Schuyler's estate and saw what she had done, they burned her house to the ground in revenge.

Women Warriors

Although women were barred from formally joining the armed forces throughout the Revolutionary War, a number of women took up arms to aid the Patriot effort. Most of these female warriors lived on the American frontier, where the bulk of the fighting during the war was not carried out between conventional armies but rather between small bands of militia and their Native American allies. Since many of these skirmishes were literally fought in settlers' backyards, countless women became involved in the war in defense of their own families and property.

Backwoods women were known for their proficiency at arms. In an era when Native American raids were still common occurrences in frontier communities, female settlers had to be able and willing to wield a gun, hatchet, or any other weapon they could get their hands on in the event of an attack. Thus, it is hardly surprising that one South Carolinian reported that Patriot frontier women in his state "talk as familiarly of sheding blood & destroying the Tories [Loyalists] as the men do."[26]

The most famous of these Patriot female warriors of the backcountry was Nancy Morgan Hart of Wilkes County, Georgia. When five heavily armed Loyalists raided Hart's home while her husband was away, she lulled

By passing as a man, schoolteacher Deborah Samson fought courageously for a year and a half as a Continental soldier.

the men with homemade whiskey, then made a lunge for their guns. Before help could arrive, Nancy had captured all of the intruders, shooting two of them in the process.

Deborah Samson: Continental Soldier

Although women participated in frontier skirmishes during the Revolution, they were strictly prohibited from enlisting in the regular army. During the course of the war, however, at least four women donned men's clothing and assumed male identities to serve as Continentals. Researchers have yet to determine the actual identity of the first woman. Historians know only that she enlisted, along with her brother, in what is now the state of Maine in 1775, and she served using a male name until the war's end. The second woman, Ann Bailey of Massachusetts, enlisted in 1777 under the alias Sam Gay. Bailey served for three weeks before her secret was discovered, during which time she was even promoted to the rank of corporal. Just how her charade was discovered is a mystery, but as soon as her identity was established, Bailey vanished. A few months later she was apprehended and brought to court. For her deceit Bailey was fined sixteen pounds and was sentenced to two months in jail. She was also formally put out of the army. Her service record states, "Discharged. Being a woman, dressed in mens cloths August 1777."[27] The third woman to enlist in the Continental Army, Sally St. Clair, was a Creole of French and African American ancestry who apparently signed up under a male alias to be near her boyfriend. The army did not discover St. Clair's gender until after her death at the British siege of Savannah, Georgia, in 1782.

Far more is known about the fourth woman to disguise herself as a man and serve in the Patriot forces, Deborah Samson, whose name is often incorrectly spelled "Sampson." At 5 feet, 8 inches, Samson was taller than the average American man when she enlisted in the army under the name of Robert Shurtliff (sometimes spelled "Shirtliff") in 1782. In an era when boys of fourteen were accepted into the armed forces, the tall and muscular twenty-two-year-old had no difficulty passing for a soldier. It was simply assumed that Shurtliff was too young to grow a beard.

A desire to escape her humdrum life as a schoolteacher in rural Massachusetts may

Anne Trotter Bailey

T he Ann Bailey who enlisted in the Continental Army as Sam Gay should not be confused with Anne Trotter Bailey, scout, messenger, spy, and fighter on the Virginia frontier. A sharpshooter and expert horsewoman, Anne Trotter Bailey aided the Patriot side during the Revolutionary War and helped to defend white settlements from Native American raids before and after the war.

have been one factor in Samson's enlistment. Yet Samson was also clearly motivated by deeply felt patriotism. Years later, in explaining her decision to fight, Samson declared that during the years preceding her enlistment, her "mind became agitated with the enquiry—why a nation, separated from us by an ocean more than three thousand miles in extent, should endeavor to enforce on us plans of subjugation, the most unnatural in themselves, unjust, inhuman in their operations, and unpractised even by the uncivilized savages of the wilderness?"[28] At last, reported Samson, "wrought upon . . . by an enthusiasm and frenzy that could brook no control . . . I threw off the soft habiliment of my sex, and assumed those of the warrior, already prepared for battle."[29]

Samson served as a Continental soldier for a year and a half. Although the Battle of Yorktown, the war's last big engagement, was fought seven months before her enlistment in May 1782, a guerrilla war was still being waged in some parts of the country between Continentals and die-hard Loyalists. Samson's company took part in several skirmishes with Loyalist units in New York. According to a sensationalized account of her military exploits written years later, during one of these conflicts Samson received a musket ball in her thigh and stoically cut it out herself to avoid detection by a doctor.

Some time later an army physician treating Samson for a fever discovered that she was an impostor. Yet, unlike the unfortunate Ann Bailey, Samson was neither fined nor imprisoned. No one knows why Samson escaped punishment for her deceit, although her proven courage on the battlefield no doubt played an important role. At any rate, Samson was given an honorable discharge from the military at West Point, New York, in October 1783.

After returning home to Massachusetts, Samson married Benjamin Gannett, a farmer, and soon had three children. Gannett, however, had trouble providing for his growing family. After another Massachusetts war hero, Paul Revere, heard about Samson's financial straits, he wrote to the state assembly requesting a pension for the debt-ridden veteran. The legislators granted Samson her military pension, the first ever given to a woman in Massachusetts, yet in a way that revealed their traditional attitudes toward women's "proper" role. In informing Samson of the pension, the assemblymen praised her feminine rectitude in the rough and crude world of the army as much as her courage under fire. Samson had, they noted, "exhibited an extraordinary instance of female heroism by discharging the duties of a faithful, gallant soldier, and at the same time preserving the virtue and chastity of her sex unsuspected and unblemished."[30]

A few years later Congress also awarded Deborah Samson a pension. When the Gannett family still could not make ends meet, Samson turned to the lecture circuit in an attempt to capitalize on public curiosity regarding her wartime role. She appeared in several northern cities and, according to an advertisement for a lecture in Boston, "equipt in complete uniform will go through the manual [military] exercises."[31]

Deborah Samson delivers a letter to General George Washington.

Samson's public speeches presented a decidedly mixed message regarding the appropriateness of her wartime actions. In one part of her Boston lecture, she defended her right to throw off traditional female roles by joining the army, proclaiming that by enlisting, "I burst the tyrant bonds which held my sex in awe, and clandestinely, or by stealth, grasped an opportunity, which custom and world seemed to deny, as a natural privilege."[32] Yet later in the same talk Samson apologized for her "unfeminine" behavior during the Revolution, declaring, "I am indeed willing to acknowledge what I have done, an error and presumption. I will call it an error and presumption because I swerved from the accustomed flowery path of female delicacy."[33] Consequently, Samson asserted, she was prepared to humbly relinquish "every claim of honor and distinction to the [male] hero and patriot, who met the foe in his own name."[34]

That Samson felt compelled to apologize for her military career indicates that her contemporaries were still deeply uncomfortable with the idea of women combatants. Indeed, curiosity—not a desire to support female participation in the armed forces—was what probably attracted most of Samson's audiences to her lectures. Yet by challenging long-accepted ideas regarding women's roles, Samson's wartime actions, like those of Darragh, Ludington, and the other female spies, messengers, and saboteurs who offered combat support to the Patriots, would someday help pave the way for the new vision of women in the military that emerged during the late twentieth century, two centuries after the Revolution.

Chapter 3:
Women Camp Followers

Although women were prohibited from formally enlisting in the military during the Revolutionary War, thousands of women attached themselves to the Continental Army from 1775 until the war's end in 1783, living and traveling with the troops. The numbers of these female camp followers varied, but historians believe that at least twenty thousand trailed after the Continental Army during the course of the war. The majority of women who tagged along with the Continentals were the wives of enlisted men. Many brought their families with them, infants and toddlers included. By accompanying their husbands to war, these women and children were following an ancient military tradition that British forces in the colonies had practiced for years. Although many Patriot commanders viewed the camp followers as irritating and burdensome, the day-to-day lives of their troops were clearly enriched by the women's presence.

Washington and the Camp Followers

The female camp followers' motives for leaving home were diverse. Some sought adventure; others simply wanted to be near loved ones. Most, however, were probably driven to accompany their husbands by economic factors. The vast majority of women camp followers came from the lowest classes of American society and were simply too poor to get by on their own. Afraid that they could not earn a subsistence for themselves or their children back home, they packed up their pots and pans and any other items that might prove useful at camp, and they set off after their men.

The predicament of these impoverished army women inspired scant sympathy from George Washington. Indeed, the fact that most were from the lower class clearly dismayed the commander in chief. A wealthy landowner and proper southern gentleman, Washington was appalled by what he viewed as the crude behavior of the women, many of whom could equal their husbands in drinking alcohol or cursing. Even some of the rank-and-file soldiers were disdainful of the low-status camp followers. Private Joseph Plumb Martin observed in his war memoirs that a "caravan of wild beasts could bear no comparison"[35] with the rag-tag group of women who trudged after his regiment. They "'beggared all description': their dialect, too, was as confused as their bodily appearance was odd and disgusting,"[36] Martin recalled.

Accustomed to associating with upper-class women who prided themselves on their elegant grooming, Washington was mortified by the camp followers' scruffy appearance. The motley band of women and children drifting behind his soldiers hurt his army's image as a professional fighting force, he fretted. Thus, when the Continental Army marched through Philadelphia in August 1777, Washington

Female camp followers had to endure the same hardships as the troops.

Women of the American Revolution

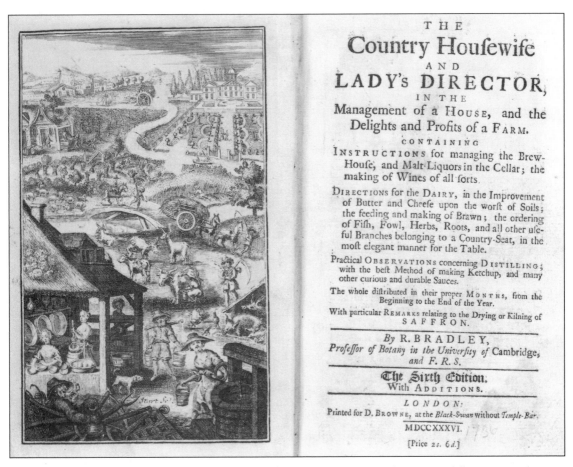

A page spread of the 1736 London publication Country Housewife. *Camp followers may have used manuals like this one during the American Revolution.*

issued an order directing the camp followers "to avoid the City entirely.... Not a woman belonging to the army is to be seen with the troops on the march."[37] While the Continentals advanced down Philadelphia's main thoroughfares, the camp followers were left to wind their way through the city's dark back alleys. According to one eyewitness, however, before the troops exited the city, the women had defiantly poured back onto its main streets to rejoin their men.

Washington's disapproval of the camp followers was not only a matter of appearances; he also objected to their presence for tactical reasons. The women, not to mention the children, dogs, chickens, and the cumbersome loads of kettles, pans, and other household items that typically accompanied them, could not help but

British Camp Followers

❧

Like the Continental Army, the British forces included a large contingent of female camp followers. Hannah Winthrop of Cambridge, Massachusetts, observed British camp women marching near her home in 1777. The wretched condition of the women shocked Winthrop. The British camp followers, Winthrop wrote,

seemed to be beasts of burthen, having a bushel basket on their back, by which they were bent double, the contents seemed to be Pots and Kettles, various sorts of Furniture, children peeping thro' gridirons and other utensils. some very young Infants who were born on the road, the women bare feet, cloathed in dirty rags, such effluvia filld the air while they were passing, had they not been smoking all the time, I should have been apprehensive of being contaminated by them.

Winthrop is quoted in Harry Ward's *The War for Independence and the Transformation of American Society.*

impair the army's mobility. The heavily burdened camp followers, Washington fumed, were an "incumbrance," a "clog on every movement."[38]

Unable to maintain a brisk pace, the women were relegated to the slowest moving section of the army—the supply and baggage wagons. Many camp followers, especially those who were pregnant or carrying young children, preferred to pile aboard the carts rather than plod along beside them. This further irritated Washington, who resented the women taking up precious space in already overloaded military vehicles. From the earliest months of the war until the Battle of Yorktown, the commander in chief issued one order after another in a futile attempt to keep the determined and, no doubt, genuinely exhausted camp followers off the army's wagons.

Yet despite his frustration with the women, Washington did not attempt to expel them from the army. Washington believed the women were useful to the Patriot cause in one vital way: He thought their presence at camp helped prevent desertions, a major problem in the Continental forces throughout the war. If the women were forbidden from accompanying their husbands or lovers, the army might "lose by Desertion, perhaps to the Enemy, some of the oldest and best Soldiers in the Service,"[39] Washington wrote candidly toward the end of the war. Allowing soldiers' wives to stay with the army was a deeply ingrained custom in both America and Europe, and Washington realized that he would have to accept the women as part of the Continental community, like it or not.

Camp Followers at Work

Although he did not refer to it in his writings about the camp followers, Washington probably recognized the women's importance in the day-to-day functioning of the army as well as in discouraging desertions. Eighteenth-century armies had virtually none of the support staff employed by modern military forces. Lacking a dependable system of auxiliary services, many soldiers relied on camp women to sew, wash, and cook for them. These jobs were, of course, the same chores that American women typically carried out at home. The "women of the army," notes historian Linda K. Kerber, "were doing in a military context what they had once done in a domestic one."[40]

Although there was little glory in this type of traditional "women's work," it was deeply appreciated by the soldiers. During the early months of the war, Washington was shocked by the appearance of his troops, many of whom were so certain that washing clothes was a female task that their uniforms were literally crusted over with filth. Little wonder, then, that many camp followers found themselves in high demand as laundresses throughout the war. Other camp followers served as seamstresses, mending uniforms for men who had never been taught to sew because, like laundering clothes, sewing was deemed to be a female chore. Cooking was another job the soldiers were happy to hand over to the camp women when possible. Many years after the war, Private Jacob Nagle still remembered his blissful anticipation of a fine breakfast that a comrade's wife was making in "the camp kittle on a small fier about 100 yards in the rear of the Grand Artilery,"[41] and his consternation when a British cannonball struck the pot, sending its contents flying.

Most camp followers were compensated for their services to the Continental Army in food, not cash. Women who worked as laundresses, seamstresses, or cooks were awarded army rations in return for their efforts. For most of the war, decisions regarding rations for camp followers were left to the discretion of local officers; typically, women received half rations and their children one-fourth rations. A few enterprising camp followers were also able to earn small amounts

This woman is demonstrating the sewing skills used by camp followers serving the troops.

of money in addition to the rations by hiring themselves out as servants, washerwomen, seamstresses, or cooks to officers. In performing this work for hire, the women were typically expected to abide by predetermined and decidedly modest fees. The orders of one Continental regiment stipulated that camp women who laundered soldiers' uniforms were to receive two shillings "a dozen for articles which they wash . . . provided they find their own soape, or one and sixpence per dozen if the soape be found for them."[42]

Nursing

Among the minority of female camp followers who received a regular salary from the military for their labor, as opposed to rations only, were army nurses. Since commanders tried to avoid giving up precious manpower for noncombat duties, camp women were widely recruited to work in the Continental hospitals.

Nursing was neither a highly respected nor a well-paid job during the eighteenth century. In the Continental hospitals, as in hospitals throughout North America and Europe, male surgeon's mates were responsible for most of the skilled tasks involved in patient care, with nurses performing the kinds of chores assigned to nurses' aides and janitors today. Nurses emptied chamber pots, bathed and fed patients, changed bedding, swept floors, and sprinkled the wards with vinegar several times a day, a procedure thought to discourage the spread of disease. For all their hard work, nurses earned only a small fraction of the pay allotted to male surgeon's mates.

Camp followers who served as nurses no doubt appreciated the opportunity to earn wages, scanty as they may have been. Yet nursing entailed significant risk, as Continental hospitals were dangerous places for patients and staff alike. Historians estimate that thousands more American soldiers died of disease than of battlefield injuries during the Revolutionary War. Crowded and poorly ventilated, Continental hospitals were excellent breeding grounds for deadly infections. Since the importance of basic hygiene technique

General Washington visits a wounded soldier. Washington hired female camp followers to nurse the wounded.

was not yet understood, illnesses were spread not only by patient-to-patient contact in the cramped wards but also by nurses and physicians who moved from one patient to another without washing their hands.

Camp followers employed in the packed, unsanitary hospitals contracted such potentially lethal diseases as putrid fever (typhoid), dysentery (severe diarrhea), white plague (tuberculosis), pleurisy (pneumonia), and the dreaded smallpox, which typically left those who managed to survive it with horrible scars. The fact that nurses, as hospital employees, could readily obtain medical treatment was of little help to them. During the Revolutionary era, medical treatment for infectious diseases was frequently more deadly than the illness itself. Favored remedies included purging the sickness out of the body with powerful emetics to induce vomiting, a practice that frequently left patients dangerously dehydrated; and bleeding the sickness out of the sufferer by cutting open a vein, a treatment that often led to excessive blood loss and death.

The Hardships of Camp Life

Camp women who never set foot in an army hospital were also at high risk for dying from disease, for the same dangerous infections that were the scourge of Continental hospitals also spread

Officers' Wives at Camp

The wartime experiences of the lower-class camp followers contrasted dramatically with those of the well-to-do officers' wives who spent time at the Continental camps. The vast majority of officers' wives were not really camp "followers" at all; rather, they were seasonal visitors who waited until the fighting season was over and the army settled into its winter quarters before joining their spouses. Visiting officers' wives like Martha Washington aided the Patriot cause by knitting and sewing for the soldiers and offering them encouragement, but their efforts were first and foremost for their husbands. Aside from providing them with some of the comforts of home, the women tried to give their husbands brief respites from their many worries by organizing card parties, dances, and other social distractions at camp.

readily through the crowded army camps. In addition to being exposed to potentially lethal illnesses, camp women braved primitive housing, arduous marches, meager rations, and all of the other miseries of army life. Like the men they followed, the women were continually plagued by a host of annoying vermin, including lice, fleas, chiggers, and bedbugs, as well as by the infamous skin condition known to Continentals everywhere simply as "the Itch," a consequence of poor hygiene combined with sleeping directly on the ground.

In addition to the difficult living conditions they endured, camp followers were subject to the same harsh discipline employed by commanders to keep soldiers in line. Women could be ducked under water, whipped, or drummed out of camp for such offenses as petty theft or prostitution. In 1778 a camp woman at Valley Forge, Pennsylvania, named Mary Johnson was sentenced to one hundred lashes and expulsion from camp after being convicted of trying to entice several soldiers to desert.

Most camp followers, however, strove to further, not undermine, the cause of the army. Despite the contempt in which the women were held by many upper-class officers, a few, like Sarah Osborn of New York, managed to earn the admiration of the Patriots' top commanders for their self-sacrificing service to the war effort. Years later, in what is believed to be the only existing autobiographical account of a female camp follower, Osborn recalled the day in 1783 when she met George Washington near Yorktown, Virginia, the site of the Revolution's last great battle. Undeterred by British bombardments, Osborn repeatedly made the perilous journey from camp to the entrenchments (fortifications) her husband and his comrades had erected some distance away to bring the men their meals. On one occasion when she "was thus employed carrying in provisions," remembered Osborn, she met General Washington, who inquired solicitously if she "was not afraid of the cannonballs?" Sarah responded to the general with poignant simplicity, saying that "it would not do for the men to fight and starve too."[43]

Camp Followers Margaret Corbin and Mary Hays

In contrast to Sarah Osborn, the majority of camp followers stayed well out of the line of fire. Convinced that women on the battlefield would distract the soldiers, Patriot officers ordered most army women to remain at camp during engagements. Commanders did, however, tolerate the presence of a small yet highly visible group of women on the battlefield. These were the water carriers, and their assistance was vitally important to the American effort. Water carriers aided the army's artillery units by hauling the cold water that the gunners urgently needed to swab out their hot cannons after each firing. Two women camp followers became legends during the Revolutionary era for assisting their cannoneer husbands in battle. They were Margaret Cochrin Corbin, and Mary Ludwig Hays, popularly known as Molly Pitcher.

Margaret Corbin, who lost both parents in an Indian attack when she was growing up on the Pennsylvania frontier, was a self-reliant woman of twenty five when she accompanied her husband, John, to war in 1776. Corbin probably performed all of the usual chores of a camp follower—washing, cooking, and sewing for her husband and perhaps for some of his comrades. She also helped John and his artillery unit in battle by carrying buckets of cold water for their cannons.

In November 1776 the British launched an assault on Fort Washington, located near New York City. John Corbin and his unit were among the Continentals assigned to defend the strategic fort. Margaret Corbin, in her post as water carrier, was standing by her husband's side

A Failed Scheme to Aid Camp Followers

❧

In 1781, one year after the women of Philadelphia contributed over two thousand shirts to the Continentals, Esther Reed's husband, Joseph, then governor of Pennsylvania, tried to arrange a similar gift of clothing for the soldiers' wives at camp in hopes of raising morale among the men and their womenfolk. Reed's address to the Pennsylvania Executive Council requesting funds for the project is quoted in Linda Grant De Pauw's *Battle Cries and Lullabies: Women in War from Prehistory to the Present:* "A new gown, silk handkerchief, and a pair of shoes, etc., would be but little expense, and I think as a present from the State would have more effect than ten times the same laid out in articles for the men," asserted Reed. But unlike his wife's earlier scheme to assist the Continentals, the governor's plan was never realized. Rejected by the Executive Council, the project to aid the camp followers was soon forgotten.

A costumed interpreter demonstrates a camp follower's skill in cooking over an open fire.

when he was struck down by a British musket ball. She immediately sprang into action, skillfully assuming her dead husband's duties of cleaning, loading, and firing the cannon. Then Corbin, too, was hit. Her arm almost severed from her body by grapeshot (small iron balls used as a charge for cannon), Corbin was captured by British troops near her husband's artillery piece. Unsure how to handle a female prisoner of war, the British first held Corbin prisoner in New York City and later transferred her to Philadelphia, finally setting her free in 1777.

Following her parole, Corbin was quartered at the army's Invalid Corps at West Point, where she remained, included on regimental muster lists in honor of her bravery, until the war's end in 1783. A few years earlier, in 1779, she had been granted a modest invalid's pension from her home state of Pennsylvania. In July of that year she also became the first woman in American history to receive an invalid's pension from the national government when Congress voted her the "same half pay drawn by a soldier in the service of these States,"[44] recognizing her valorous service to her country. Twenty years later, at the age of forty-nine, Corbin died in the small town of Highland Falls, New York, and was buried there in an unmarked grave. Yet Margaret Corbin's military exploits were not entirely forgotten; stories about her bravery on the battlefield continued to be handed down in Highland Falls long after her death. Finally, in 1926, during the sesquicentennial of American independence, a female patriotic organization had Corbin's remains transferred to a military cemetery at West Point, where they were placed beneath a monument commemorating her deeds at Fort Washington a century and a half earlier.

A second camp follower and water carrier who became renowned for her actions in battle was Mary Hays. Dubbed "Molly Pitcher" after the war, she was celebrated for her valor at the Battle of Monmouth in New Jersey on June 28, 1778. On that brutally hot day, Hays, the wife of a Pennsylvania cannoneer, hauled pail after pail of water up the hillside where her husband and his crew were positioned, both to quench the men's thirst and to cool their dangerously overheated cannons. When Hays's husband suddenly fell unconscious at his cannon, probably a victim of heatstroke, Hays wasted no time in taking his place. Throughout the rest of the battle she competently swabbed, loaded, and fired her disabled spouse's gun.

Mary Hays remained with the army as a camp follower until the war's end. Widowed soon after the Revolution, she had a brief second marriage, then lived out the rest of her days in her hometown of Carlisle, Pennsylvania. In 1822, when she was seventy-eight years old, Hays's military contributions were officially recognized at last when she was awarded a pension by the state of Pennsylvania "for services rendered"[45] to her nation.

Despite her heroic actions at the Battle of Monmouth, Mary Hays developed a tarnished reputation during the century following her death. Reputed to be a heavy drinker with a penchant for chewing tobacco and cussing, Molly Pitcher seems to have been just the sort of rowdy, lower-class camp follower who so mortified Washington during the war. During the mid-nineteenth century, reports historian Lincoln Diamant, a group of genteel Philadelphia ladies allegedly "thanked their lucky stars when certain contemporary testimony was brought to their attention, and caused them to abandon the idea of erecting a civic monument to Molly's memory."[46] That "contemporary testimony," Diamant believes, probably came from a veteran of the Battle of Monmouth, Joseph Plumb

When Molly Pitcher's cannoneer husband collapsed in battle she took his place, swabbing, loading, and firing the cannon.

Martin, whose derogatory comments about the camp followers accompanying his regiment are quoted above. Published more than fifty years after the battle, Martin's memoirs describe a female camp follower with a raunchy sense of humor whom many of the book's readers took to be Hays:

> One little incident in the heat of the cannonade would be unpardonable not to mention. A woman attending with her husband at his artillery piece the whole time, and in the act of reaching for a cartridge and having one of her feet as far before the other as she could step, a cannon shot from the enemy passed directly between her legs, without doing any other damage than carrying away all the lower part of her petticoat [underskirt]. Looking down with apparent unconcern, she observed that it was lucky it did not pass a little higher, for in that case it might have carried away something else—and continued her occupation.[47]

It is impossible to know what spurred Mary Hays and Margaret Corbin to risk their lives on the battlefield since they failed to leave behind a written account of their motives. Perhaps they were driven more by personal loyalty to their spouses than a well-thought-out commitment to American independence. On the other hand, as historian Carol Berkin points out, they, like the thousands of other camp women who shared in the miseries and adventures of army life with their menfolk, "may also have entered the military camps with loyalty to a political cause as well articulated as their husband's."[48] What can be said with certainty is that Hays, Corbin, and the other female camp followers of the Continental Army made vital contributions to the Patriot cause by supporting and assisting the men whom they accompanied to war.

Chapter 4:
Patriot Women on the Home Front

❦

Despite the valor of women camp followers and soldiers like Margaret Corbin and Deborah Samson, the most significant contribution made by American women to the Patriot cause was probably not on a battlefield or in an army camp but rather at home. For every woman who accompanied her husband or lover to war, many more remained at home alone, tending the family farm or business. These women kept the economy of their young nation alive by planting and harvesting food crops and producing and trading other goods needed by both the military and civilian populations. In attempting to fulfill these vital economic duties, American women confronted an array of daunting challenges, ranging from inflation to shortages to threats to the safety of their property, families, and themselves from enemy troops.

Facing Wartime Inflation and Scarcity

Runaway inflation combined with a nearly worthless currency made it difficult for women all over America to provide for their families while their male relations were at war. Throughout the Revolution, spiraling prices and devalued paper money ate up the hard-earned savings of countless Americans. By 1778 it was said that four months of a soldier's pay in continentals, as the paper money issued during the war was known, could not purchase even one bushel of wheat. "Our money will soon be as useless as blank paper,"[49] Abigail Adams wrote in 1777 from the family farm in Massachusetts to her husband, future president John Adams, then serving in Congress at Philadelphia.

Adams and thousands of other women across America undoubtedly would have recognized many of the economic concerns and frustrations recounted in a broadside published in Marblehead, Massachusetts, in 1779. The broadside's anonymous author, who identified herself simply as "A Daughter of Liberty living in Marblehead," described the hardships facing the women of her seaside town, left on their own to cope not only with a devalued currency but also with grave shortages of salt, fuel, bread, and other necessities:

It's hard and cruel times to live,

Takes thirty dollars to buy a sieve . . .

For money is not worth a pin,

Had we but salt we've any thing,

For salt is all the Farmer's cry,

If we've no salt we sure must die.

We can't get fire nor yet food,

Takes 20 weight of sugar for two

Rendered nearly worthless by inflation, little could be purchased with Continental currency.

Women of the American Revolution

On farms like this one in Pennsylvania, resourceful women made do with what few goods were available.

foot of wood,

We cannot get bread nor yet meat,

We see the world is nought but cheat . . .

I now have something more to say,

We must go up and down the Bay.

To get a fish a-days to fry,

We can't get fat, were we to die,

Were we to try all thro' the town,

The world is now turn'd up-side down.[50]

The scarcities lamented by Marblehead's "Daughter of Liberty" created a great deal of anxiety for women all over the country during the Revolutionary War. Salt shortages were particularly worrisome, for salt was far more than a seasoning for eighteenth-century

Sending Men to Battle

❦

Although numerous private letters and diaries testify to the reluctance with which women parted with their husbands, sons, and lovers during the Revolutionary War, throughout the conflict American newspapers carried articles about Patriot women enthusiastically sending their men off to fight. Many of these articles are difficult to take literally and may well have been invented by propagandists hoping to promote military enlistment and bravery on the battlefield. In one account published in the *Pennsylvania Evening Post* in 1776, a grandmother from New Jersey supposedly tells her sons and grandsons: "My children, I have a few words to say to you, you are going out in a just cause, to fight for the rights and liberties of your country; you have my blessings. . . . Let me beg of you. . . that if you fall, it may be like men; and that your wounds may not be in your back parts." The account of the patriotic grandmother appears in 'History Can Do It No Justice': Women and the Reinterpretation of the American Revolution," by Linda K. Kerber, in *Women in the Age of the American Revolution,* edited by Ronald Hoffman and Peter J. Albert.

Americans. In the absence of refrigeration, it was also used to preserve fish and meat. Forced to find a substitute for the scarce mineral, some women soaked their meat in a caustic solution extracted from walnut ashes, a preservation method that surely did nothing to enhance the flavor of the food.

A variety of other wartime shortages also compelled women to improvise as best they could. For example, housewives substituted thorns for scarce pins and maple syrup or the sweet residue from boiled cornstalks for hard-to-come-by sugar and molasses. Faced by a scarcity of yarn and thread, one resourceful South Carolina woman later recalled that she "used to darn my stocking with the ravellings of another."[51]

Facing Confiscation and Plunder

Wartime shortages had many causes, ranging from British efforts to cut off America's foreign trade to the absence of thousands of male workers from farms and workshops. Also contributing to home front shortages were the confiscation of crops, fuel, and other provisions by British, and occasionally American, forces, and plundering by armed raiders who claimed loyalty to one side or the other.

Patriot women complained bitterly of losing precious fuel and other provisions to the British troops they were compelled to quarter in their homes during military occupations. One disgruntled Long Island housewife reported that the Hessians (German mercenaries) she was forced to house during the British occupation of New York "take the fence rails to burn, so that the fields are left open, and the cattle stray away and are often lost; burn fires all night on the ground, and to replenish them, go into the woods and cut down all the young saplings, thereby destroying the growth of ages."[52]

British troops traveling through an area also plundered homes and farms, making off with cattle and pigs, raiding vegetable cellars, and foraging corn, apples, and other produce from private fields and orchards. Apparently viewing foraging as a punishment for rebel families as well as a convenient way of obtaining much-needed provisions, many British officers made little effort to stop their men from looting.

American troops, who suffered greatly during the war from shortages of staples, also sometimes confiscated food and other supplies from families living in war zones. In a 1786 petition to Congress requesting compensation for losses she incurred during the war, Rachel Wells claimed that her New Jersey farm had been plundered not only by Redcoats but also by Patriot soldiers on the march.

Women had good reason to fear losing property to looters other than soldiers in the regular armies. The confusion of the war years promoted widespread plundering by roving bands of thieves who claimed to be aligned with the Patriots or the Loyalists. Women made especially easy targets for these armed and ruthless gangs.

In the southern backcountry, where guerrilla warfare between Patriot and Loyalist militia was common, the almost constant partisan fighting brought about a collapse of law and order in many communities, and robbery was rampant. Groups of thugs whose loyalty to either side in the conflict was dubious at best roamed the countryside, stealing horses and cattle, boats and carts, crops and slaves, jewelry, and even clothing. The "havoc" created by the robbers "is not to be described," reported one South Carolinian in 1779: "Great Numbers of Women and Children have been left without a 2nd Shift of Clothes. The furniture which they could not carry off they wantonly broke, burnt, and destroyed."[53]

Houses in the southern backcountry were sometimes plundered by bandits associating themselves with either the Loyalist or Patriot cause.

With their husbands, fathers, and brothers off fighting, many southern women were forced to face the bandits by themselves. Left alone on her plantation near Charleston, South Carolina, with a few female relatives, Eliza Wilkinson related her terror one day in 1780 when marauders broke into her house and took "every thing they thought valuable or worth taking,"[54] including the women's gowns, earrings, and wedding rings. Years later Wilkinson vividly remembered the emotional trauma of being robbed at gunpoint in her own home:

The whole world appeared to me as a theater, where nothing was acted but cruelty, bloodshed, and oppression . . . where the lives and property of the innocent and inoffensive were in continual danger, and the lawless power ranged at large. . . . We could neither

Women of the American Revolution

eat, drink nor sleep in peace; for as we lay in our clothes every night, we could not enjoy the little sleep we got. . . . The least noise alarmed us; up we would jump, expecting every moment to hear them demand admittance. In short, our nights were wearisome and painful; our days spent in anxiety and melancholy.[55]

It should be noted, however, that women were not always the victims of wartime plundering; in a few cases, they were the perpetrators. In the southern backcountry, bands of thieves associating themselves with the Loyalist cause sometimes included a female or two. According to one eyewitness, the women bandits rode "the best Horses and Side Saddles, and Drest in the finest and best cloaths that could be taken from the inhabitants as the [British] army marched through the country."[56]

Facing Physical Violence

Looting was not all that American women living in war zones dreaded. The threat of physical violence, and particularly rape, from the troops who roamed nearby caused enormous anxiety for countless women. Their fears were justified: Rape appears to have been a common practice during the Revolutionary War. Although some of the assaults were committed by American soldiers, the existing evidence indicates that most were carried out by British and Hessian soldiers. During the Revolution, as in countless other wars throughout history, rape "had political implications,"[57] historian Joan R. Gundersen points out. Since Patriot women were the wives, daughters, and sisters of the enemy troops, some Redcoats may have considered the assault of American women as just another means of humiliating and asserting dominance over their foes.

In Connecticut, New York, and New Jersey, there were a number of documented rapes of girls and women involving British and Hessian soldiers. In late 1776 women on Staten Island near New York City lived in constant terror of assault by the royal occupying forces. Despite repeated complaints to British officials regarding attacks on islanders by soldiers, commanders made little effort to prevent the assaults. Indeed, one high-ranking officer, Lord Rawdon, exhibited no sympathy whatsoever for the terrorized women and girls, even indicating in a letter to his uncle in England that he found their plight amusing. "The fair nymphs of this isle are in wonderful tribulation," he wrote. "A girl cannot step into the bushes to pluck a rose without running the most imminent risk of being

Policing Hoarders

I n Boston and other cities during the Revolutionary War, some women attempted to put a stop to what they believed to be the deliberate hoarding of scarce commodities such as coffee, sugar, molasses, and wool by local merchants. In a letter to her husband, Abigail Adams recounted an incident in 1777 in which a group of Boston women pressured a "stingy" merchant into lowering his prices on coffee. Throughout the entire proceedings, reported Adams, a large group of men "stood amazd silent Spectators." Adams is quoted in Phyllis Lee Levin's *Abigail Adams: A Biography*.

It was rumored that an eminent, wealthy, stingy Merchant . . . had a Hogshead of Coffe in his Store which he refused to sell to the committee under 6 shillings per pound. A Number of Females some say a hundred, marched down to the Ware House and demanded the keys, which he refused to deliver, upon which one of them seazd him by his Neck and tossed him into the cart. Upon his finding no Quarter he deliverd the keys, when they tipd up the cart and discharged him, then opend the Warehouse, Hoisted out the Coffe themselves, put it into the truck and drove off.

ravished. . . . We have the most entertaining court-martials every day."[58]

Although Patriot propagandists eagerly seized upon and publicized any stories of alleged enemy atrocities, including rape, assaults on American women by royal troops were probably underreported during the war. Women who had been attacked were often hesitant to report the crime to the authorities. The risks associated with disclosure were simply too great. If their ordeal became public knowledge, the rape victims who had already endured so much might find themselves facing stigmatization and ostracism from their own communities as well. As a report prepared for Congress in 1777 on the rape of American women by Redcoats explained, although the government had "authentic information of many instances of the . . . ravishment of married and single women . . . such is the nature of that most irreparable injury that the persons suffering it, though perfectly innocent, look upon it as a kind of reproach to have the facts related and their names known."[59] A Patriot in New Jersey also recognized this especially cruel aspect of the crime, observing that "against both Justice and Reason We Despise these poor Innocent Sufferers"; consequently, "many honest virtuous women have suffered in this Manner and kept it Secret for fear of making their lives miserable."[60]

The truth of the New Jersey man's words are poignantly illustrated in a story related by a Continental officer in 1780. Upon entering the small town of Connecticut Farms, New Jersey, shortly after it was raided by British and Hessian soldiers, the officer encountered a sobbing girl. In response to his questioning, the despondent girl would tell him only "that she was ruined and wished never again to be spoken to."[61] The officer later learned that she had been assaulted by seven or eight different soldiers of the royal forces.

Women Hold Their Own

Faced with the daunting economic and psychological burdens of a home front war, some women sent emotional letters to their soldier-husbands begging them to come home. In 1778 a Continental officer complained,

> Not a Day passes . . . but some Soldier with Tears in his Eyes, hands me a letter from his Wife Painting forth the Distresses of his family in such strains

as these, "I am without bread, and cannot get any. . . . My Children will Starve, or if they do not, they will freeze, we have no wood, neither Can we get any, *Pray Come Home.*"[62]

Letters like those described by the Continental officer prompted some American men to desert, or at least to refuse to reenlist. Yet many husbands and fathers would not or could not avoid military service during the Revolutionary War. They had no choice but to entrust their wives or daughters with managing the family farm or business for months and often years at a time. And although for some Patriot women the absence of their male relations brought only defeat and despair, countless others handled their new responsibilities with great success. Many even began to relish the challenge of being in charge of their family's financial affairs for the first time, gaining an unprecedented sense of confidence in their own judgment and abilities as the months and years went by.

In examining the wartime correspondence between Patriot soldiers and their wives, historian Mary Beth Norton notices a pattern in many of the letters that reveals women's changing sense of their economic role and importance. In the earliest letters, women wrote to their husbands about "your

The Terrors of a Home Front War

When fighting erupted between British and American soldiers at Lexington and Concord, Massachusetts, in April 1775, the women of eastern Massachusetts became the first American females to experience the grim realities of a home front war. "We were roused from the benign Slumbers of the season," reported Hannah Winthrop of Cambridge, Massachusetts, to her friend Mercy Otis Warren on April 19, 1775, "by beat of drum and ringing of Bell, with the dire alarm that a thousand of the Troups of George the third were gone forth to murder the peaceful inhabitants of the surrounding villages." As the fighting approached the outskirts of her hometown, Winthrop viewed in horror "the glistening instruments of death, proclaiming by an incessant fire, that much blood must be shed, that many widow'd & orphan'd ones be left." Winthrop's letter is quoted in Carol Berkin's *First Generations: Women in Colonial America*.

farm," eventually progressed to calling it "ours," and by war's end referred to it as "my farm."[63] Similarly, at the outset of the war many men gave their wives highly specific orders regarding business and family affairs, but their later correspondence commonly included statements of confidence in their wives' ability to act independently, such as, "I . . . Leave all to your good Management"; "Apply [the money] to such as you think proper"; borrow "any Sums you may choose, for providing things necessary & comfortable for yourself & . . . Family for the approaching Season, in doing which I am sure you will use the greatest discretion."[64]

With their husbands away, Patriot women found themselves shouldering a variety of jobs traditionally thought of as male duties. Aside from managing the family money, many took up fieldwork for the first time in their lives, planting and harvesting crops and caring for livestock. As Azubah Norton, a Connecticut farmwife, declared, after 1777 her husband "was out more or less during the remainder of the war, so much so as to be unable to do anything on our farm. What was done, was done by myself."[65] Despite a greatly increased workload and the challenges posed by wartime inflation and a devalued currency, some women, especially in New England, where the fighting ended early, were able to turn a small profit from farming during the Revolution. "For many more, there was satisfaction in simply preserving the family's farm or business through the long economic crisis,"[66] writes Carol Berkin.

Mary Fish Silliman of Connecticut, whose husband and grown son were away for long periods during the Revolution, found comfort in her many wartime responsibilities on the family farm not only because they gave her a new faith in her own abilities but also because they provided a much-needed distraction from her worries about her absent loved ones. As Silliman's biographers, Joy Day Buel and Richard Buel, write,

> The extra burden of work, though it taxed her endurance, was not without psychological benefits. . . . Though her loneliness and her fear grew as the days of [her husband's] absence lengthened, so did her competence to do the work that filled her waking hours, and . . . in that work she found a prop and stay to her sanity.[67]

Abigail Adams: Patriot "Farmeress"

The most famous Patriot woman left to maintain the household economy while her husband was off aiding his country was Abigail Adams. With John Adams absent for most of the war serving in various official capacities, Abigail took charge of the large family farm in Braintree, Massachusetts. Like countless other Patriot women, although at first overwhelmed by her new duties, she quickly learned to manage.

Early in the conflict, John Adams wrote his wife from Philadelphia: "I . . . entreat you to rouse your whole attention to the Family, the stock, the Farm, the Dairy. Let every Article of Expense which can possibly be spared be retrenched. Keep the Hands attentive to their Business, and [let] the most prudent Measures of every kind be adopted."[68] Determined to meet her husband's expectations of her, Abigail replied that she hoped "in time to have the Reputation of being as good a Farmeress as my partner has of being a good Statesman."[69] Abigail succeeded admirably, managing not only to keep the farm going during the war but also to keep the family out of debt, despite having to cope with myriad troubles ranging from spiraling inflation to labor shortages to a dearth of wool and cotton for clothing. "I hardly know how I have got thro these things," she wrote to John at one point regarding her many pressing responsibilities, "but

Abigail Adams ran the business of her farm from this kitchen.

it gives me great pleasure to say that they are done because I know it will be an Ease to your mind."[70] John's reply reflected his pride in his wife's achievements: "I begin to be jealous, that our Neighbors will think Affairs more discreetly conducted in my Absence than at any other time," he teased, adding on a more serious note that their friend James Warren had recently informed him "that my Farm never looked better, than when he last saw it, and that Mrs. [Adams] was like to outshine all the Farmers."[71]

During the Revolution families across America depended on their female members to shoulder tasks absent husbands and fathers could no longer perform. In addition to their numerous domestic chores, women raised crops, cared for livestock, repaired fences, purchased equipment, and managed the family

finances, all the time coping with inflation, looting, physical violence, and other
hardships engendered by a home front
war. Their contributions to the Patriot
cause may not appear as dramatic as
those of the war's female spies, messengers, or fighters. Yet because these determined and resourceful home front heroines kept their fledgling nation's economy functioning during difficult and
uncertain times, their assistance was surely as crucial.

Chapter 5:
Loyalist and Pacifist Women

The Revolutionary War was not only a crusade for independence; it was also a civil war. Throughout the conflict men and women in each of the thirteen former colonies remained loyal to the British Crown, although Loyalists (or Tories, as the Patriots called them) were most numerous in Georgia, the Carolinas, and the mid-Atlantic states. Loyalists came from all economic, ethnic, and occupational groups. However, of the estimated 20 percent of America's white population who were active Loyalists, most fell into one of several different categories: British-appointed officials; Anglican clergymen (because the Anglican leadership was in England); merchants whose trade depended on British connections; certain cultural and ethnic minorities, particularly the Scots; and some backcountry southerners who disliked the local Patriot leadership.

Loyalist women faced all of the same burdens of a home front war as their Patriot sisters, including runaway inflation, a nearly worthless currency, short-ages of staple products, and the threat of physical violence from soldiers stationed or fighting nearby. In addition to bearing these hardships, however, Loyalist women also had to cope with persecution and plundering by their Patriot neighbors, confiscation of their property by Patriot officials, and, in some cases, forced exile.

Persecution and Confiscation

Since thousands of Loyalist men left home to serve in Loyalist militias or the British army, many Loyalist women found themselves in charge of the family farm or business during the Revolutionary War. As historian Janice Potter-MacKinnon points out, although Patriot wives also had to assume unprecedented responsibility for their households during the Revolution, there was a vital difference between Loyalist and Patriot families:

> While Patriot men were away from home either fighting the war or

helping their cause in other ways, most could return home without fearing for their lives. Many Loyalist women, however, were left behind enemy lines. It was, therefore, difficult and dangerous for their husbands to come home and risk being charged with treason, mobbed, or even killed. Thus, in practice, Loyalist women were even more likely than their Patriot counterparts to have to make decisions on their own.[72]

In addition to having to rely more on their own judgment, Loyalist women compelled to live behind enemy lines confronted other challenges not experienced by their Patriot counterparts. For Tory women, the threat of violence against themselves, their families, and their property was ever-present. This held particularly true for women whose husbands openly served in Loyalist militias or the British army. Many found themselves facing angry mobs bent on

In this cartoon, Loyalists are being slaughtered by rebels represented by Native Americans. Loyalist women were often subject to threats and violence that their Patriot counterparts did not experience.

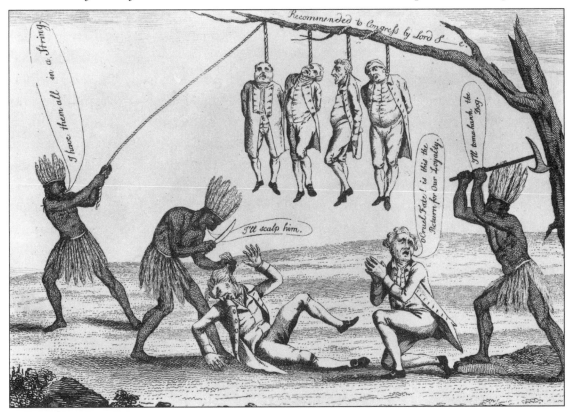

ransacking and robbing their homes and farms. The disorder of the war years encouraged plundering and willful destruction of property generally. But Loyalist families, who were often isolated from other community members and even relatives because of their political sympathies, were prime targets for vandals and thieves, and Tory women left at home alone were particularly easy prey.

Countless Loyalist women were stripped of property during the war not by irate mobs or roving bands of thieves, however, but by Patriot officials. Patriot authorities justified the confiscation of houses, land, and valuables such as furniture and jewelry belonging to Loyalists because Tories were the enemies of the American government. Early in the war state assemblies and the Continental Congress approved acts allowing specially created committees to seize and sell the estates of Loyalists tarnished as traitors. This not only satisfied any desire the Patriots might harbor to punish the Tories, but it also provided a source of revenue for hard-pressed local governments and political committees.

Some men who joined Loyalist or British forces held out the hope that their political decisions would not cost their wives dearly at the hands of Patriot officials. Women, especially mothers of young children, they trusted, would

receive special treatment based on their gender and parental responsibilities. As one Loyalist wrote to his wife shortly after joining the British army, "Surely [a Patriot] has not got so barberously mad as to Mollest or hurt a poor innocent woman and still more Innocent poor Children."[73]

State assemblies and local Patriot committees chose not to treat the wives of Loyalists as independent actors, however, apparently reasoning that since women were expected to defer to their spouses, they would naturally adopt their husbands' political beliefs. Consequently, thousands of Loyalist women found themselves at the mercy of unsympathetic officials who argued that if a male head of household aided the enemy, then not only he, but his wife as well, was no longer entitled to the family holdings. British and colonial legal custom lent support to this stance. Under the traditional concept of "coverture," married women were considered to be one person with their husband—when they gave up their single status, they also relinquished all independent identity before the law.

Among the thousands of female Loyalists who suffered as a consequence of the popular assumption that married women were politically as well as legally one with their husbands was Abigail

Lindsey of New York. When her husband, John, joined a Loyalist regiment and went to Canada in 1780, Abigail stayed behind to run the family farm. No sooner had John left than the local Patriot committee showed up at Abigail's doorstep demanding all the livestock and every chair, table, and chest in the house "because her Husband was gone to the British."[74] Convinced that she had no choice but to submit to the committee's demands, Abigail handed over "1 horse, 2 cows, and 10 sheep" along with "all the furniture,"[75] then packed up her children and the few household items she had left and headed for Canada and her husband.

A Loyalist Wife Fights Back: Grace Growden Galloway

One Loyalist wife who dared to stand up to Patriot confiscators was Grace Growden Galloway of Philadelphia. The strong-willed daughter of a wealthy Philadelphia merchant, Grace was married to Joseph Galloway, a prominent lawyer and Loyalist. After British forces seized control of Philadelphia, Joseph was rewarded for his loyalty by being appointed police superintendent. In the summer of 1778 the Continental Army reclaimed Philadelphia, and Joseph fled to British-occupied New York City, taking the couple's daughter with him. Despite her husband's pleas to join

Florence Cooke: A Patriot Wife Fights for Her Rights

In a petition to the South Carolina legislature in 1783, Florence Cooke, the wife of a carpenter who had been convicted of treason, strongly asserted her right to be considered as an independent actor from her Tory spouse. In her petition Cooke stated that since she had been a loyal Patriot throughout the war, the state's recent confiscation of her family's estate was unjust. "Your Petitioner is not only innocent of any crime, but if a sincere affection for the independence and freedom of her Country, avowed and testified in the worst of times, be any Merit, she flatters herself she had some to plead," wrote Cooke, whose petition was ultimately accepted. Cooke's petition is quoted in Linda K. Kerber's *Women of the Republic: Intellect and Ideology in Revolutionary America*.

them, Grace obstinately stayed behind to protect the family property from confiscation. At the very least, she hoped to save valuable real estate that she had inherited from her father some years before.

As the wife of a prominent Tory, however, Grace Galloway never stood a chance with her husband's Patriot foes. Anger against the British and their Loyalist supporters ran high among the citizens of Philadelphia in 1778. The city had suffered much vandalism under royal control, and, far worse, scores of American prisoners of war had died from starvation or disease in squalid British prisons during the occupation.

Just one day after her husband left town with the British army, Patriot officials informed Grace Galloway that the family house was being confiscated because of Joseph's treason. "I would not go out unless by the force of a bayonet,"[76] Grace told them defiantly. Yet despite her determined court battle to retain the family property, in the end Grace found herself evicted from her home and stripped of her furniture, carriage, and jewels. Worst of all, she could not even prevent the confiscation of her inheritance from her father, which was deemed to be part of her husband's estate since, according to the custom of coverture, a wife's property remained under her spouse's control throughout his lifetime.

Her health broken by the long and frustrating legal fight, Grace Galloway died in 1782 at the home of friends, a bitter and defeated woman. Shortly before her death, she wrote to her daughter, now in England with Joseph, informing her that they had lost everything. "I care little for the world," the once vivacious Grace confided in her only child: "Indeed, my dear, I am not like the same person in any thing but my unbounded affection for you."[77]

Loyalist Husbands/ Patriot Wives

Although Grace Galloway avoided airing her political opinions in public, it is evident from her diary that she agreed with her husband's Loyalist views. Not every woman married to a Loyalist shared his beliefs, however. Nor did every woman married to a Patriot adopt his opinions, despite the widely accepted assumption that a woman naturally followed her spouse's political lead.

An example of an openly Patriot woman married to a Tory was Elizabeth Graeme Fergusson of Pennsylvania. Fergusson's husband, Hugh, was a fervent Loyalist who fled America for England after the British evacuated Philadelphia in 1778. Disgusted with

Hugh's decision to abandon his country, Elizabeth defiantly stayed behind. Yet despite her outspoken support for the Patriots, the state of Pennsylvania still confiscated all of the family property because of her husband's treason. Only after a long and persistent campaign was Elizabeth able to convince authorities to reverse the confiscation. Toward the end of her life, Elizabeth, who never reconciled with her husband, wrote a poem in her diary blasting those who

Deem Woman made alone for mans Control,

Like Mahomets fair ones void of noble Soul

As Birds or Insects for a Boy to please

They torturd Subjects made [for] their Lords to teize (tease).[78]

One woman who rejected her husband's Patriot views in favor of Loyalism was Elizabeth Henry of South Carolina. When Elizabeth refused to keep her Loyalist sentiments to herself, her husband, an ardent supporter of American independence, threw his wife out of the house. According to Linda Grant De Pauw, another Patriot man married to a Loyalist woman tried to squelch political quarrels in their home by painting the words "No Tory Talk Here,"[79] over the family mantelpiece.

Women Who Actively Aided the Loyalist Cause

Evidence indicates that Elizabeth Henry did not only speak out in support of the British cause; she also spied for it. Loyalist women, like their Patriot counterparts, took great risks to aid their side, carrying dispatches, scouting, spying, and recruiting troops.

Perhaps the most effective Loyalist female spy of the Revolutionary War was Ann Bates, a Pennsylvania schoolteacher. Bates began spying for the British in 1778. Posing as a peddler selling needles, combs, and other items to soldiers and camp followers, Bates traveled from one Continental Army camp to another. As she peddled her wares, she noted the size of the forces and the type and number of their artillery pieces. Like Patriot spies such as Lydia Darragh or Dicey Langston, Bates's gender apparently worked in her favor, for she attracted little suspicion from the Patriots during the three years she served as a British agent.

Although Bates managed to avoid detection by the Patriots, another Loyalist woman who assisted the Redcoats was less fortunate. New Yorker Lorenda Holmes conveyed dispatches to and from British army camps during the summer

Peggy Shippen Arnold

❦

One of the most famous female Loyalists was Peggy Shippen Arnold, the wife of General Benedict Arnold. Descended from a prominent Philadelphia family, the attractive and charming Peggy married Arnold when she was just nineteen and he was a Patriot military hero. Soon after the marriage, Arnold resolved to defect to the British. No one knows with certainty if Peggy played a role in Arnold's decision, but Peggy did have close friends on the British side, including Major John Andre, a British officer and spy. After Peggy introduced her husband to Andre, the two men hatched a plot to deliver West Point, New York, where Arnold was commanding officer, to British forces. After their scheme was discovered by the Patriots, Arnold fled behind British lines and Peggy was left to confront General Washington alone. Peggy claimed to be unaware of the plot, but she soon joined Arnold in exile after incriminating letters she had written to Andre were made public.

of 1776. Finally apprehended by Patriot authorities, she was stripped of her clothing and was forced to face an angry mob. Perhaps out of respect for her gender, however, the mob jeered Holmes but did not physically harm her. In applying for a military pension from the British government after the war, Holmes noted that she "received no wounds or bruises from them only shame and horror of the mind."[80]

Humiliated but undeterred, Holmes continued to collaborate with the British, helping Loyalists wanting to enlist in the British army to sneak through Continental lines. Soon Holmes found herself back under arrest, and this time the Patriots were not as lenient. In her petition for a royal military pension, Holmes reported that one of her captors ordered her to remove her shoes, then took "a shovel of Wood Coals from the fire and by mere force held Your Memorialists right foot upon the Coals until he had burnt it in a most shocking manner and left Your Memorialists saying that he would learn her to carry off Loyalists to the British Army."[81] After being cautioned never to return, Holmes was allowed to get herself behind British lines. The Patriots' harsh treatment of Holmes had the desired effect: Not only did she give up spying, but she soon left her homeland altogether.

Flora MacDonald

The most famous female Loyalist to provide assistance to the British military was probably Flora MacDonald, who emigrated from Scotland to North Carolina in 1774 with her husband, Allan. A celebrity in her homeland, MacDonald had once helped to save the life of "Bonnie Prince Charlie," a Scottish royal who organized a doomed uprising against England.

In North Carolina, Flora and her husband were highly respected members of the colony's large Scottish community. When the Revolutionary War began, the MacDonalds used their considerable influence among their fellow Scots to help the British forces. It may seem strange that Flora, who had become famous for aiding a royal rebel against the British in her homeland, should take Britain's part in its struggle with the Americans. But the MacDonalds, in common with other North Carolinian Scots, disliked their colony's Patriot leadership, whom they viewed as power-hungry upstarts. Based on past experience in their homeland, they may also have feared serious reprisals from the British if they sided with the revolutionaries. Consequently, the MacDonalds worked hard to encourage Scots in their area to take up arms in support of the royal army. Flora spoke often at the recruiting rallies organized by her husband, and her status as one of Scotland's most revered heroines no doubt attracted many of her listeners to the British side.

With Flora's assistance, a Loyalist unit composed primarily of Scottish immigrants was soon formed, and in 1776 they met the enemy in battle near North Carolina's Cape Fear River. The results were disastrous for the Scottish militia-

A Scottish immigrant, Flora MacDonald, fought for the Loyalist cause, eventually losing her goods, house, and plantation.

men. Allan MacDonald and more than half of his unit were taken prisoner by the larger Patriot force. While Allan languished in prison, the MacDonalds' house and plantation were looted and vandalized. In 1777, after her husband was freed as part of a prisoner exchange, Flora and her family departed America for good, sailing first for Canada, and from there back to Scotland.

Exile

Like Flora MacDonald, thousands of other Loyalist women fled their homes and communities during the Revolutionary War. Many sought refuge in British-held areas such as New York City, which remained under royal control for nearly the entire war. From there and other British-controlled ports, many joined Loyalist husbands or other family members in sailing to Great Britain, British colonies in the Caribbean, and Canada, which was by far the most popular destination for American exiles. By 1785, two years after the war's end, as many as one hundred thousand Loyalists had left the country, either voluntarily or because they had been banished by law. The majority would never return.

Following the war, a number of Loyalist women who resettled in Canada and elsewhere petitioned the British government for relief. Most

had been widowed as a consequence of the Revolution. Among the many sad stories related by the petitioners was that told by Polly Dibblee of Stamford, Connecticut, whose husband, Filer, was a prominent lawyer and Loyalist. Five times the Dibblee family was forced to move because of Filer's Loyalism. At last, they abandoned their homeland for New Brunswick, Canada. Seriously in debt and reduced to living in a crude log cabin, Filer sank into depression. Finally, one March day in 1784, "whilst the Family were at Tea," Polly reported, "Mr. Dibblee walked back and forth in the Room, seemingly much composed: but unobserved he took a Razor from the Closet, threw himself on the bed, drew the Curtains, and cut his own Throat."[82]

For Polly Dibblee and her family, life in Canada was more difficult than ever after Filer's death. The family's cabin burned down twice, and Polly and her children often went hungry. Yet tens of thousands of Loyalist exiles and their families, particularly those who settled in Canada, were more fortunate, putting down roots in their new homes and, in time, even prospering. Others managed to drift back to their homeland during the decades following the war, able for the most part to blend quietly into their old communities, their controversial actions during the war forgiven or forgotten.

Pacifist Women: The Case of the Quakers

The Loyalists were not the only group in Revolutionary America who disagreed with the Patriots' decision to break free of British rule. A number of pacifistic Christian sects also challenged the Patriots' declaration of independence from the Crown by refusing to support the American war effort in any way. Quakers (as members of the Society of Friends were popularly known), Shakers, Moravians, Mennonites, and Amish were among those colonists who objected to the rebellion because of their belief that all warfare went against God's commandments. Of these sects, the Quakers were by far the largest, wealthiest, and most influential, especially in the state of Pennsylvania, which had been founded in the 1600s by the English Quaker William Penn.

Taking the attitude that anyone who was not with them was against them, many Patriots found the neutrality of the Quakers and other pacifistic religious groups unacceptable. In most states, pacifists were exempted from serving in the military themselves, but they were still expected to hire substitutes to fight in their place. Fines, confiscation of personal property, and imprisonment faced those who failed to comply. In some places, pacifists who refused to sign oaths

The Shakers: Controversial Pacifists

In 1774 Ann Lee, a recent immigrant from England, founded a new religious sect in New York that her contemporaries dubbed the Shakers since its members often physically shook during emotional services. Known to her followers as Mother Ann, Lee claimed to have the power to work miracles. Soon her sect had attracted a dedicated following in New York and New England. When war broke out, Patriot leaders in the Northeast became alarmed by Lee's strongly pacifistic teachings. Denouncing the Patriots as anti-Christian, Lee said that people could not both follow Christ and fight a revolution. In 1780 Lee was imprisoned for several months for trying to dissuade American citizens from answering militia calls. Undeterred, Lee resumed her antiwar preaching after her release.

A Quaker woman addresses a meeting.

actually aided the enemy in any way. Among them was Thomas Fisher, whose wife, Sally, was nearly eight months pregnant. Sally Fisher found the uncertainty and anxiety of the forced separation hard to bear: "I feel forlorn & desolate, & the World appears like a dreary Desart, almost without any visible protecting Hand to guard us from the ravenous Wolves & Lions that prowl about for prey,"[83] she wrote in her diary a week after Thomas was taken away. For the next seven months she and the other wives lobbied persistently to get the exiles back; those who could do so even journeyed to George Washington's winter quarters in Valley Forge to petition the commander in chief directly. Only after two of the detained men sickened and died were Thomas Fisher and the other surviving Quaker exiles allowed to return home.

Not even the surrender of the British forces at Yorktown, Virginia, in 1781 ended Patriot persecution of pacifistic Quakers in Pennsylvania and elsewhere, as the letters of Anne Rawle, a twenty-three-year-old Quaker from Philadelphia, reveal. After the Continental Army retook Philadelphia in 1778, Rawle's stepfather was accused of aiding the royal occupying forces and was sent into exile in New York City. Rawle stayed on in the family's Philadelphia home with her sister and several other female relatives. As Rawle

of allegiance or pay special war taxes to the American government could also be fined, jailed, or even exiled.

In the autumn of 1777, just before the British conquest of Philadelphia, seventeen of the city's most prominent Quaker citizens were exiled to frontier Virginia for refusing to support the American war effort and for suspected Loyalism, although there was no proof that they had

Women of the American Revolution

explained in a letter to her mother in New York dated October 25, 1781, when reports of the British surrender reached Philadelphia, citizens were urged to place candles in their windows as a sign of support for the Patriots. Anyone who refused was considered a traitor and could expect to have their windows broken or worse. When Rawle and her Quaker relatives declined to participate in the illumination, she wrote, an angry crowd surrounded their house, broke the shutters and the glass of the windows, and were coming in. . . . Not knowing what to do, we ran into the yard. . . . We had not been there many minutes before we were drove back by the sight of two men climbing the fence. We thought the mob were coming in thro' there, but it proved to be Coburn and Bob Shewell [Quaker friends of the family], who called to us not to be frightened and

Quakers were persecuted by the Patriots for their pacifistic beliefs.

fixed lights up at the windows, which pacified the mob, and after three huzzas they moved off. . . . Coburn and Shewell were really very kind; had it not been for them I really believe the house would have been torn down.[84]

As were the majority of Loyalists who drifted back to the new nation from exile in Canada or Britain, during the years following the Revolutionary War most Quakers were forgiven by their community members for failing to support the Patriots. Nonetheless, the Quaker denomination would never completely overcome the unpopularity it had suffered during the Revolution. Nor would American, and especially Pennsylvania, Quakers ever fully regain the economic, social, and political power they had once enjoyed.

Chapter 6:
Native American Women

❧

On the dawn of the Revolutionary War, perhaps two hundred thousand Native Americans lived in the area now comprising the United States from the Atlantic Ocean west to the Mississippi River. The majority belonged to one of three different cultural groups: the Algonquian-speaking tribes of the Northeast, the so-called Five Civilized Tribes of the Southeast, and the powerful Iroquois Confederacy, which was centered in northern New York.

Although there were differences in the traditions and lifestyles of the various Native American groups residing east of the Mississippi at the time of the Revolution, the tribes shared one important characteristic: A century and a half of European settlement in America had significantly affected them all. Before Europeans arrived in the New World, Native Americans survived entirely by fishing, hunting, gathering wild plants, growing food crops, and by using tools, utensils, and weapons they had fashioned

themselves. After European settlement, Native Americans relied increasingly on manufactured goods provided to them by white settlers in return for furs or land. Old ways of hunting and craftsmanship were forgotten as they became more and more dependent on European knives, kettles, needles, cloth, and guns.

When the Revolutionary War broke out, the Native Americans' close ties with the white population made it inevitable that they would be pulled into the conflict. Whether their tribe supported the Patriots or the British, or tried to stay neutral, Native American women throughout eastern North America were touched by the war in significant and, as it would turn out, irreversible ways.

Native American Women on the Eve of the Revolution

Although Native American life changed considerably with the introduction of European technology, on the eve of the

Revolutionary War the division of work between the sexes remained much the same as it had been for centuries. In addition to trading with the settlers, men's responsibilities continued to center on hunting and warfare, and women's duties included planting and harvesting crops, gathering wild foods such as berries and nuts, cooking, and making clothing and moccasins.

The women's central role in raising food crops gave them an important position in eastern Native American societies, particularly within the powerful Iroquois Confederacy. Iroquois clans were matrilineal, meaning that kinship

Clan mothers played powerful roles in agriculture and food distribution in Mohawk villages.

Women of the American Revolution

and inheritance were based on the mother's family line. Women owned their village's crops and fields collectively. Within some nations in the confederacy, such as the Mohawk, clan mothers were selected each year to direct the women's agricultural endeavors and to distribute the food they raised at festivals and councils. Because of their economic importance to the tribe, the opinions of clan mothers were respected, even on political and military matters. When a chief died, clan mothers chose his successor. In times of war, clan mothers were allowed to determine the fate of captives taken in battle, and when warrior's councils disagreed on military issues, clan mothers were sometimes given the final say. Since they supervised the use of farmland and therefore controlled much of their people's food supply, clan mothers could also influence a decision not to go to war at all simply by refusing to provide warriors with the necessary field rations.

Molly Brant: Mohawk Clan Mother and Loyalist

When the Revolutionary War began, one Native American woman who did a great deal to determine her people's role in that conflict was a Mohawk clan mother named Konwatsi'tsiaienni (meaning "Someone Lends Her a Flower"), or Molly Brant, as she was known within the white community. Brant's influence was so great that it extended even beyond her own nation to include other nations within the mighty Iroquois Confederacy.

During the Revolutionary War, both British and Patriot commanders recognized the vital strategic importance of the Native American communities living on the fringes of white settlements, particularly the warlike Iroquois. "To preserve the friendship . . . of these Indians became a major aim of the diplomacy and military strategy of both sides,"[85] writes historian Barbara Graymount. In the high-stakes tug-of-war between the Crown and the Patriots for Native American support, however, the British had significant advantages. Many Native Americans believed that an alliance with the British would go further than one with the colonists in ensuring that they continued to receive the trade goods on which they had come to rely. Also working in the Crown's favor was the colonists' response to the royal Proclamation of 1763, which prohibited whites from settling on Native American lands west of the Appalachian Mountains. Deeply resentful of the limitations placed on them by the proclamation, many colonists openly flaunted its provisions, erecting illegal

Molly Brant in Exile

❧

Despite losing much of her property to Patriot looters, Brant fared better than most Loyalist Iroquois during the Revolutionary War. While they crowded into makeshift shelters around Fort Niagara, Brant moved into a comfortable house built for her by the British directly outside the fort. For her assistance to the Crown during the Revolution, after the war Brant was awarded a royal pension of one hundred pounds annually—"the highest sum given to any Indian," according to Barbara Graymount in her book *The Iroquois in the American Revolution.*

settlements on Native American territory. Little wonder, then, that tens of thousands of Native Americans believed that their interests would be better served by aiding the British rather than the Patriot side.

Yet despite the compelling reasons for supporting the Crown in its struggle with the colonists, the single most powerful Native American group on the continent, the Iroquois Confederacy, was at first determined to stay out of the white men's squabbles. Not until Molly Brant decided to use her considerable influence within the confederacy to promote the British cause were the Iroquois drawn into the war.

According to historian Janice Potter-MacKinnon, Brant "was a woman of great prestige in her nation and throughout the Confederacy."[86] "One word from her goes farther with [the Iroquois] than

a thousand from any white man without exception,"[87] noted a British official in New York. Brant's lofty status was derived not only from her position as a clan mother and as the descendant of a high-ranking Mohawk family but also from her relationship with a white man—Sir William Johnson, the longtime British superintendent of Indian affairs for the northern colonies. Brant, whose parents were close friends of Johnson, learned to speak English fluently as a child, probably in a Christian missionary school. When she was in her early twenties she became romantically involved with Johnson, and although there was no legal marriage, the couple remained together for nearly twenty years until Johnson's death in 1774.

Moving back and forth between cultures, Brant retained close ties with her tribe while adopting much of the

European lifestyle. Outfitted in the latest European fashions, Brant devoted much of her time to running Johnson's luxurious New York home, a Georgian-style mansion with a formal English garden. Although her official title was housekeeper to Sir William, Brant had a number of servants and African American slaves to clean and cook for her and the eight children she had with Johnson.

Brant's common-law husband commanded enormous respect among the Iroquois people, who viewed him as their trusted advocate within the British regime. Even after Johnson's death shortly before the start of the Revolutionary War, Brant continued to enjoy a devoted following among her fellow Iroquois based on her long-time association with Johnson probably as much as on her traditional role as clan mother.

A War Against Women

By 1777 Brant, with the assistance of her warrior brother Joseph, had convinced the Mohawk and two other Iroquois nations, the Seneca and the Cayuga, to aid her late consort's country. The Patriots quickly felt the results of Brant's successful recruiting among the Iroquois. Vicious raids were launched against American settlements on the New York frontier, and at the Battle of Oriskany in August 1777, Patriot forces suffered heavy casualties when they were ambushed near Fort Stanwix, New York, by Loyalists and their Mohawk and Seneca allies. According to some accounts, it was Molly Brant herself who informed the ambushing party of the whereabouts of the American troops.

In retaliation for the Oriskany ambush and the violent frontier raids, the Continental Congress sent an expedition under the command of Major General John Sullivan to New York to destroy Britain's Iroquois allies. Crashing straight into the heart of Iroquois country, Sullivan and his men took revenge on the Iroquois warriors' wives and children even more than on the warriors themselves. Ordered by their commander to leave nothing edible in their path, the invaders torched entire settlements, destroying mile upon mile of corn, bean, and squash fields ripe for the harvest. The Patriots' scorched-earth campaign "waged war directly on the Indian women who planted and tended these crops,"[88] notes historian Joan R. Gundersen. Left without shelter or food stores for the winter, the destitute Iroquois women and their children suffered terribly. Thousands were forced into exile, taking refuge in miserable huts hastily erected around the British-held Fort Niagara. At Niagara they died in droves from disease, malnutrition, and exposure.

Chores being performed in a Mohawk village; planting and tending crops, as well as food preparation, was women's work.

One of the Iroquois women who made her way to Fort Niagara was Molly Brant. When rumors of her involvement in the Oriskany ambush began to circulate, Brant gathered up her children, servants, and slaves and fled for the British stronghold. Soon after, the Patriots looted her estate in New York, making off with "sixty half Johannesses [Portuguese gold coins], two Quarts full of silver, several Gold Rings, Eight pair Silver Buckels, a large Quantity of Silver Broaches, Together with several silk Gowns."[89] According to one account,

children of the looters mocked Brant by parading around in her gowns while their mothers and fathers loaded their wagons with Brant's belongings and vandalized her house.

Yet Brant and other Iroquois women with ties to the British were not the only female Native Americans who suffered as a consequence of the Revolutionary War. Just as the Revolution was a civil war for America's white inhabitants, the conflict likewise pitted Native American against Native American, particularly Iroquois against

Iroquois. Influenced by a charismatic rebel missionary who had lived among them for years, two nations in the Iroquois Confederacy, the Oneida and the Tuscarora, chose to support the Patriots during the war. Oneida and Tuscarora women paid dearly for their leaders' decision. Following the destructive Sullivan expedition against Loyalist Iroquois villages, vengeful Mohawk warriors under the command of Molly Brant's brother Joseph and other pro-British Iroquois raided Oneida and Tuscarora villages. As was the case in the Sullivan raids, crops and food stores as well as homes were burned, once again leaving the tribes' women and children to bear the brunt of the enemy's rage.

By the end of the Revolutionary War, the tribes' divided loyalties had irrevocably weakened the once powerful Iroquois Confederacy. Like their white counterparts, thousands of Iroquois Loyalists fled to Canada during and directly after the war, leaving their homeland behind forever. For those who stayed, including even the Oneida and the Tuscarora tribes who had cast their lot with the Patriots, the end of British rule only brought more white encroachment on their lands, as the ambitious young American nation pushed ever farther into Iroquois country.

Mary Jemison: A White Woman Among the Iroquois

Captured from her home on the Pennsylvania frontier and adopted by Native Americans when she was still a girl, Mary Jemison witnessed firsthand the suffering and decline of the Iroquois during the Revolutionary War, later recording her memories of those turbulent years in her autobiography. Although Native Americans sometimes tortured and killed their prisoners of war, many hostages, especially women and children like Jemison, were adopted by their captors and treated as equal members of their villages and clans. Raised by a loving adoptive family, Jemison soon came to cherish her new life, finding her chores as a Native American woman less burdensome than her day-to-day work in the white settlement from which she had been abducted. Indian women, she noted in her memoirs, worked at their own pace and were freed from such tedious and time consuming chores as "spinning, weaving, sewing, [and] stocking knitting."[90]

Although given complete freedom of movement by her adoptive tribe, Jemison did not try to return to the white community. Instead, she married a Seneca warrior, remaining with his people until she was well into her eighties. In her autobiography she recalled the

Jane McCrea and the Iroquois

The highly publicized murder by Iroquois warriors of Jane McCrea, a young white woman, generated a great deal of anti-British as well as anti-Indian feeling among the people of New York during the Revolutionary War. McCrea was engaged to a Loyalist enlisted in the British army and was on her way to visit her fiancé at Fort Edward, New York, in 1777 when she was ambushed by an Iroquois war party. Unaware that she was actually pro-British, the Iroquois split McCrea's skull with a tomahawk and, according to some accounts, scalped her. Although not a Patriot herself, McCrea became a martyr to the rebels' cause when, despite pleas from local Patriot officials, the British commander refused to punish the guilty Iroquois for fear of jeopardizing his country's alliance with their people.

impact of the Revolution on the pro-British Seneca, including their losses at the Battle of Oriskany against the Patriots: "Our Indians alone had thirty-six killed, and a great number wounded. Our towns exhibited a scene of real sorrow and distress, when our warriors returned and recounted their misfortunes."[91] But the loss of life at Oriskany marked only the beginning of wartime misery for Jemison's tribe, as her recollections of the destructive Sullivan expedition and its aftermath reveal:

> Sullivan and his army arrived at the Genessee river, where they destroyed every article of the food . . . that they could lay their hands on. A part of our corn they burnt, and threw the remainder into the river. They burnt our houses, killed what few cattle and horses they could find, destroyed our fruit trees, and left nothing but the bare soil and timber. . . .

> The succeeding winter . . . was the most severe that I have witnessed since my remembrance. The snow fell about five feet deep, and remained so for a long time; and the weather was extremely cold, so much so, indeed, that almost all the game upon which the Indians depended for subsistence perished, and reduced them almost to a state of starvation through that and three or four succeeding years. . . . Many of our people barely escaped with

their lives, and some actually died of hunger and freezing.[92]

In relating the tribulations of her adopted people during the Revolution, Jemison told a story about two Oneida brothers that dramatically illustrates the divisive effect of the war on the Iroquois community. One brother fought for the Patriots, Jemison reported, while the other broke with his tribe and joined the British. When the Loyalist Oneida captured his Patriot brother in battle, he urged his fellow warriors to show no mercy toward his kinsman, according to Jemison, "Though you have merited death and shall die on this spot, my hands shall not be stained in the blood of a brother. *Who will strike?* Little Beard . . . struck the prisoner on the head with his tomahawk, and dispatched him at once."[93]

Nancy Ward: Cherokee Friend to the Patriots

In the Southeast of the Five Civilized Tribes, as in the Iroquois-dominated Northeast of Mary Jemison and Molly Brant, Native American women and their families were unavoidably drawn into the divisiveness and brutality of the Revolutionary War. This held particularly true for the Cherokee, one of the most powerful southern nations. After

Cherokee warriors urged on by the British attacked Patriot frontier settlements in the Carolinas and Virginia in 1776, American militias struck back with overwhelming force, ravaging Cherokee homes, crops, and food storehouses. As in Iroquois country, women may have been the war's chief victims in the Cherokee nation, as scores of homeless and starving mothers and wives were left to somehow provide for their children in the absence of warrior husbands and fathers. According to one Patriot militiaman, Cherokee families "were reduced to a state of the most deplorable and wretched, being obliged to subsist on insects and reptiles of every kind."[94]

One Cherokee woman who sought to protect her people from the destructive consequences of involvement in the white men's war was Nanye'hi (meaning "One Who Goes About"), or Nancy Ward. Cherokee women, like their Iroquois counterparts, controlled their people's agricultural fields and enjoyed an important position in their matrilineal clans. If a Cherokee woman displayed unusual wisdom or bravery, she might be named a *Ghighua,* or Beloved Woman, entitling her to prepare warriors for battle, determine the fate of prisoners of war, vote in the Council of Chiefs, and act as a peace negotiator.

American militias ravaged Cherokee homes, crops, and food storehouses.

Two decades before the Revolutionary War, when she was a young widow, Nanye'hi was made a Beloved Woman of the Cherokee for taking up her slain husband's gun in battle and helping his fellow warriors defeat their enemy. A few years later, Nanye'hi, who had been taught to speak English by Christian missionaries, married a white trader named Bryant Ward and assumed the name of Nancy Ward.

As Cherokee war parties backed by the British were raiding communities on the Carolina and Virginia frontiers, Ward sought to use her status among her people to ensure peaceful relations with the white settlers near her home in present-day Tennessee. On at least two occasions she managed to thwart Cherokee attacks on white communities on the Watauga River by sending warnings to the settlers of the planned raids. According to some accounts, she also pled for peaceful coexistence between Cherokee and whites at tribal war councils, but there is no surviving record of her speeches. In 1781 Ward, in her role as Beloved Woman, acted as a negotiator in peace talks between the Cherokee and representatives of the American government. Ward's eloquent plea to the American officials

for a peaceful solution to differences between her people and white settlers in Tennessee has been preserved. Apparently unaware that women held a very different position in white society than in Cherokee society, Ward urged the commissioners to take the treaty back to "your women" for them to approve: "We are your mothers; you are our sons. Our cry is all for peace; let it continue. This peace must last forever. Let your women's sons be ours; our sons be yours. Let your women hear our words."[95]

Yet if Nancy Ward clearly believed that promoting peace between her people and

Elizabeth Zane:
Teenage Heroine of Fort Henry

O ne young white woman who took part in the fighting on the American frontier between Patriot settlers and British-supported Native Americans was sixteen-year-old Elizabeth Zane. Elizabeth and her family lived just outside Fort Henry in present-day West Virginia. When a force of Shawnee and other Loyalist Native Americans attacked Fort Henry, Elizabeth's family sought refuge within the stockade. Soon the besieged settlers had run out of gunpowder. Something had to be done,

and Elizabeth boldly volunteered to fetch the gunpowder stored in her house beyond the fort walls. When the warriors saw a girl running away from the fort, they held their fire. On Elizabeth's return trip with the gunpowder, however, the men realized what she was up to and fired repeatedly at her. Amazingly, Elizabeth made it back to the stockade safely. With the gunpowder she brought, the settlers were able to hold out until reinforcements could arrive.

the American settlers was essential for Cherokee survival, she nonetheless objected strongly to turning over large tracts of tribal land to the Americans as a means of trying to ensure their goodwill. The raids of 1776 on Patriot frontier settlements had cost the Cherokee nation dearly, not only because of the Americans' retaliatory attacks on their villages and fields, but also because of the punitive treaties their chiefs had been compelled to accept in their wake. By 1777 Cherokee chiefs had signed away 5 million acres of land to the American government, ceding all territory east of the Blue Ridge Mountains in North Carolina, Virginia, and Tennessee. Ward spent the decades following the war urging her people to avoid relinquishing any more of their dwindling land supply to the new American regime. "The pressures were too great, however,"[96] notes Linda Grant De Pauw, and by the time of her death in 1822, Ward herself had been uprooted from her longtime village of Chota to a new location farther south in Tennessee after the American government claimed the territory where her hometown stood.

Like Molly Brant, Nancy Ward would die in forced exile from her own home. For Brant, Ward, and countless other Native American women and their families, the Revolutionary War was a no-win situation. Whether they cast their lot with the Patriots or the British, or attempted to remain neutral, the war ultimately brought hardship and loss to all Native Americans east of the Mississippi River. Within fifty years of the Revolutionary War, with the election of the renowned Indian fighter Andrew Jackson to the presidency, the U.S. government would adopt a formal policy of removing all Native Americans in the East from their lands. The new Indian policy was remarkably successful. By the mid-1830s all of the various Native American groups who had played a role in the Revolutionary War (other than those who had fled to Canada) had been forcibly relocated west of the Mississippi, excluding a tiny minority who remained behind on reservations.

Chapter 7:
African American Women

In 1775, of the approximately five hundred thousand African Americans living in British North America, all but perhaps twenty-five thousand were enslaved. By law, slaves were property that their masters could use as they desired; they could be bought, sold, or beaten at their owners' will. When war broke out between Britain and her colonies, African Americans saw in the conflict an opportunity to escape the horrors of bondage. Thousands of slaves, male and female alike, tried to attain their freedom by joining the British, and others aligned themselves with the Patriot cause, drawn by the Patriots' rhetoric of liberty and natural rights.

African American Women on the Cusp of the Revolution

Life was hard for the female slaves of British North America prior to the Revolution. Since slave marriages were not legally binding, women could be sold away from their husbands at their mas-

ter's whim. They also had to live with the constant fear that their children could be torn from them at any time, for few masters showed any concern for keeping enslaved mothers and their offspring together. Typically, enslaved women toiled for their owners from dawn to dusk, with Sunday their only day of rest. The work they did varied according to whether they lived in an urban or a rural area, on a small farm or a plantation. Urban female slaves spent their days cooking, sewing, or cleaning for their masters, and slave women on small farms usually mixed domestic chores with fieldwork. On the great tobacco and rice plantations of the South, where the majority of African American slaves lived, most women labored in the fields. No clear division was made between the work of male and female slaves on Revolutionary-era plantations. Like their male counterparts, female slaves spent exhausting days tending and harvesting crops under a merciless sun. They also engaged in other forms of hard physical labor, from felling trees to chopping wood to digging ditches. At nightfall, they returned to the crowded, crude cabins of the slave quarter, where they did their best to make a home for themselves and their children.

Facing Shortages and Separations

When war came to America in 1775, the lives of America's enslaved women became even harder. All classes of American women were affected by shortages during the Revolutionary War. Yet wartime scarcities of food and cloth were felt most deeply by enslaved women, especially in the South, where the bulk of the fighting took place after 1778.

"Forced to make do with less in the way of food, clothing, and other basic supplies, white Southerners considered the daily needs of their slaves to be a low priority,"[97] notes historian Jacqueline Jones. Throughout the South, wartime disruptions meant that slaves failed to receive

Slaves harvest cotton under a merciless sun; wartime shortages made slaves' lives even more difficult.

Women of the American Revolution

Sacrificing for the Patriot Cause

❦

Among the African American women who aided the Patriot cause was an anonymous free woman from Philadelphia. During the British occupation of Phila-delphia in 1778, a white Philadelphian noted with obvious admiration the woman's efforts on behalf of Patriot prisoners of war:

Having received two hard dollars for washing, and hearing of the distress of our prisoners in the gaol [jail], went to market and bought some neckbeef and two heads, with some green, and made a pot of as good broth as she could; but having no more money to buy bread, she got credit of a baker for six loaves, all of which she carried to our unfortunate prisoners, who were much in want of such supply. She has since then paid the baker, and says, she never laid out money with so much satisfaction. Humanity is the same thing in rich or poor, white or black.

The story about the self-sacrificing African American woman is quoted in Elizabeth Evans's *Weathering the Storm: Women of the American Revolution*.

even the meager supplies of extra clothing their masters ordinarily issued to them each winter. Looting of fields, livestock, and food stores on plantations by armies and marauding bands loosely associated with one side or the other added greatly to the slaves' suffering. The toll these depredations took on the slaves' normally scanty diet reduced "the poor Negroes to a starving condition in many places hereabout,"[98] a British officer stationed in South Carolina noted in his diary.

The turmoil of the war years brought increased emotional as well as physical suffering to enslaved women in all parts of British America. Many white families fled their homes when enemy forces approached, hauling their slaves with them. For African Americans living in urban areas, where few households had more than three or four slaves, this often meant that husbands and wives were separated since few enslaved couples shared the same owner. Wartime disorder also divided slave families in rural areas, especially on southern plantations. Because slaves were considered valuable property and plundering was rampant in the

South, notes historian Sylvia R. Frey, slaves were compelled "to live with the constant fear of abduction by roving partisan bands or by one of the belligerents."[99]

Escape

The disorder of the war years brought many hardships to enslaved African Americans. Yet wartime disruptions also brought unprecedented opportunity to escape from bondage. Some slaves took advantage of the wartime chaos to flee the British colonies altogether, making their way to Spanish Florida, Mexico, or Canada. Others sought refuge with Native American groups or established their own small communities in the wilderness. The vast majority of those who ran, however, ran to the British.

Early in the war, the British sought the backing of the colonies' African Americans, particularly in the South. Soon after the battles at Concord and Lexington, Lord Dunmore, Virginia's royal governor, proclaimed that all slaves owned by Patriots would be welcomed into the British army and freed in exchange for their services. Four years later, in 1779, General Henry Clinton, the British commander in chief in America, issued another order offering freedom to "every Negro who shall desert the Rebel Standard."[100]

Dunmore's and Clinton's announcements triggered mass escapes on plantations throughout the South, with women making up as many as two-fifths of the runaways. Before the war, most slaves faced a long and arduous journey to freedom, a trip that would have been all but impossible for women with children in tow. Consequently, the vast majority of runaways before 1775 were male. With royal forces camped nearby during much of the Revolution, many female slaves, even those burdened with numerous children, were willing to pursue Britain's offer of freedom. Of the twenty-three slaves whom Thomas Jefferson recorded as having "joined British"[101] in the farm book he kept for his Virginia estate, twelve were women, and one took three children with her. Seventeen slaves fled from George Washington's Virginia estate for British encampments, including "Lucy, a woman about 20 years old. Esther, a woman about 18 years old. Deborah, a woman about 16 years old,"[102] according to plantation records.

Staying with the British

No record exists of Lucy's, Esther's, or Deborah's experiences with the British army. It is likely, however, that the time they spent with the Redcoats was filled with misery and hardship. "Few slave

Seventeen slaves fled George Washington's Mount Vernon estate for the British encampments.

women found a haven behind British lines,"[103] notes Jones. Had royal officials been motivated by strictly humanitarian concerns in offering freedom to enslaved African Americans, the women's experiences might have been different. But the British were far more interested in using the escaped slaves to further their own interests than they were in helping them. As historian Ray Raphael explains, above all, "Royal officers wanted slaves for the labor they might per-form—and to deprive the rebels of that labor."[104]

Both male and female runaways who sought refuge with the British were worked hard by those from whom they sought protection. Women escapees were expected to serve the British military in a variety of ways, from making musket cartridges to laboring in army hospitals to acting as personal servants to officers. Officially, most of these women received wages for their work. Once they reimbursed the army for their food, however, the women seldom found themselves with any money left over.

Both food and shelter for the African Americans who attached themselves to the royal forces were inferior to that provided to British soldiers, and in times of shortage, the runaways' already meager rations were the first to be cut back. "Overworked and undernourished, they fell easy prey to disease,"[105] notes Frey. Although large numbers of British and Patriot soldiers also died of disease during the war, mortality rates among African Americans in British army camps were significantly higher than those for white soldiers or camp followers on either side. Illnesses such as typhus, dysentery, and smallpox claimed the lives of countless African American women who fled to the British in search of freedom.

Medical care for sick African Americans, like rations, was woefully inadequate in the British encampments. On at least one occasion, ill escapees were simply abandoned by the Redcoats. In 1776, hoping to contain an epidemic of smallpox among African Americans staying with British troops in Virginia, Lord Dunmore ordered that the stricken runaways be removed to an island in the Chesapeake Bay. When American forces captured the island, a Patriot soldier described "the deplorable situation of the miserable wretches left behind" by the royal troops:

> Many poor Negroes were found on the island dying of the putrid fever; others dead in the open fields; a child was found sucking at the breast of its dead mother. In one place you might see a poor wretch half dead making signs of water, in another, others endeavoring to crawl away from the intolerable stench of dead bodies by their sides.[106]

Freedom Achieved and Denied

Even for those African American women who managed to survive the perils of life in a British army camp, the dream of freedom often proved fleeting. By the end of the Revolution, many women escapees found themselves back in bondage. Like their male counterparts, female runaways with Loyalist masters were returned to their owners by the British army whenever possible. Other female runaways were denied their freedom after the war not because their owners were pro-British but because they had been taken as contraband by royal officers. A number of these women were sold by their new masters to planters in the British West Indies. On

Conditions on Caribbean sugar plantations, where some female runaways were shipped, were even worse than on American soil.

the sugar plantations of the Caribbean islands, the women's working and living conditions were usually even worse than they had been on the American plantations where most had once toiled.

Although many female runaways never realized their goal of freedom, thousands did manage to escape bondage permanently after joining the British. More than ten thousand slaves were evacuated from America on British ships at the end of the war, of which perhaps half were women and children. Most of these exiles faced a very uncertain future. The majority of the former slaves were settled by the British government in segregated communities in Nova Scotia. Unlike the white Loyalists who fled to Canada after the Revolution, however, few of the former slaves who sailed to Nova Scotia on British ships were awarded grants of land by the

Crown. Tragically, the malnourished and disease-ridden black communities in Nova Scotia were also forced to endure repeated attacks by hostile whites living nearby.

Phillis Wheatley: Patriot Slave and Poet

Although a far greater number of African Americans cast their lot with the British than with the Patriots, as many as five thousand black men served in the Continental Army. That number included free black volunteers attracted by Patriot rhetoric of liberty and equality, or in some cases, by the army's promise of regular wages, as well as slaves who had fled Loyalist owners.

Some enslaved African American women also saw in the Patriot cause their best hope for freedom and a better life. The most famous black female Patriot was the slave and poet Phillis Wheatley. Abducted from Africa by slavers in 1761 when she was just seven years old, Phillis was purchased by John Wheatley of Boston to be a maid for his wife, Susannah. Immediately taken with the girl, Susannah was intrigued by Phillis's remarkable intellect. "Without any assistance from school education, and by only what she was taught in the family," John Wheatley later wrote of the young slave, "she, in sixteen months'

time from her arrival, attained the English language . . . to such a degree as to read any, the most difficult parts of the Sacred Writings, to the great astonishment of all who heard her."[107]

In a society that assumed that blacks were intellectually inferior to whites, the Wheatleys viewed Phillis as a sort of natural wonder. Treating her with a degree of respect that perhaps no other African American slave had ever enjoyed, they encouraged her hunger for learning and her aptitude

Phillis Wheatley, America's first published black poet.

Women of the American Revolution

Phillis Wheatley on George Washington

Wheatley's poem in honor of George Washington was highly laudatory of the new commander in chief, as these verses from the last stanza illustrate:

A crown, a mansion, and a throne

that shine,

With gold unfading,

WASHINGTON! be thine.

Although himself a slave owner, Washington's letter of thanks to Wheatley for her poem was respectful and appreciative:

I thank you most sincerely for your polite notice of me, in the elegant lines you enclosed; and however undeserving I may be of such encomium and panegyric [a formal expression of praise], the style and manner exhibit a striking proof of your poetical talents; in honor of which, and as a tribute justly due to you, I would have published the poem, had I not been apprehensive, that, while I only meant to give the world this new instance of your genius, I might have incurred the imputation of vanity.

The poem and Washington's letter are reprinted in Sidney Kaplan and Emma Nogrady Kaplan's *The Black Presence in the Era of the American Revolution*.

for writing poetry. Although she was responsible for performing certain household chores, Phillis spent much of her time at her studies, which included literature, science, mathematics, and history. By the time she was a teenager, she was one of the best-educated females in the colonies.

Phillis was probably also one of the most politically aware young women in America. In 1770, when she was just seventeen, Phillis wrote a poem that clearly revealed her strong Patriot views. In the poem Phillis extolled the memory of eleven-year-old Christopher Seider of Boston, who was killed by a Tory official during an anti-British protest: "In heaven's eternal court it was decreed / Thou the first martyr for the cause should bleed / To clear the country of the hated brood / He whet his courage for the common good."[108]

At first, Phillis's poems circulated only among the Wheatleys' relations and close friends. With the publication of her poem honoring the popular religious leader George Whitefield late in 1770, Phillis's fame spread. In 1772 John Wheatley arranged for a collection of Phillis's poems on nonpolitical themes to be published in London. The following year Phillis traveled to London to be on hand when the book came off the press. There she was invited to the homes of the city's social elite, whose "benevolent conduct" toward her filled her "with astonishment," Phillis reported.[109]

Back in America, Phillis Wheatley's poetry was also attracting the attention of many prominent people, particularly leading Patriots. When George Washington assumed command of the Continental Army in 1775, Wheatley boldly wrote to the new commander in chief, enclosing a poem she had composed in his honor. Washington wrote back, thanking Wheatley and praising her poetic skills. A few months later the poem was published in the *Pennsylvania Magazine,* whose editor introduced the verses to his readers as "*written by the famous* Phillis Wheatley, *The African Poetess.*"[110]

By the time her ode to Washington was published, Phillis Wheatley was a free woman. The Wheatleys had liberated her shortly after her return from London, probably bowing to widespread public criticism in Britain regarding her continued bondage. For a time, Wheatley stayed on with John and Susannah as a paid servant. By 1778, however, both were dead, and Wheatley had lost the only home she had known for seventeen years as well as her chief sponsors. That year she married John Peters, a free African American. Their life together in war-torn Boston was filled with disappointment and economic difficulties. With her most important patrons dead and most of her other white sponsors too immersed in the war to take notice of her, Wheatley sank into obscurity and debt. She continued to write, but she could not find a printer willing to publish her new poems.

By 1784, a year after the war's end, John Peters was gone—probably to debtor's prison—and Wheatley had been reduced to working as a servant in a cheap boardinghouse. Her health and spirit broken, Wheatley died that year at the age of thirty-one. The Patriots' most ardent female African American supporter and America's first published black poetess was buried in an unmarked grave. Not a single mourner attended her funeral.

Elizabeth Freeman Sues for Her Liberty

Although antislavery themes were virtually absent from Phillis Wheatley's poetry, in 1774 she wrote a letter to a friend, the Native American missionary Sampson Occom, in which she denounced slavery as being contrary to Patriot ideals. It did not "require the penetration of a philosopher" to comprehend that the Patriots' "cry for liberty" could not live side by side with the "disposition for the exercise of oppressive power over others," she wrote angrily to Occom.[111]

For Wheatley, as for countless other African Americans, Patriot rhetoric regarding the right of all people to enjoy liberty hit painfully close to home. Inspired by the ideal of natural rights put forth in the Declaration of Independence, some slaves in the North, where such legal actions were permissible, sued for their freedom in state courts during the war. For these slaves, the surest route to freedom seemed to lie not through escape but through the Patriot-controlled court system.

The best known of the enslaved African Americans who sued for their freedom during the Revolutionary War was a woman: Mum Bett, or Elizabeth Freeman. When she was still an infant, Mum Bett was purchased by John Ashley, a prominent Massachusetts lawyer. For the next four decades she toiled in the

Antislavery Sentiment and the Revolution

❧

During the Revolutionary War opposition to slavery grew rapidly in the northern states. The Quakers had been the first important group to attack the institution during the mid-1700s, but their influence was mostly limited to Pennsylvania and New Jersey. The Revolutionary-era emphasis on natural rights attracted new recruits to the antislavery cause across the North as the contradiction between the Patriots' insistence on their own rights and their willingness to ignore the rights of the enslaved became too obvious to be ignored. A year before the Battles of Concord and Lexington, Abigail Adams expressed her own discomfort with slavery in a letter to her husband: "I wish most sincerely that there was not a slave in the province. It allways appeared a most iniquitious [vicious] Scheme to me—fight ourselves for what we are daily robbing and plundering from those who have as good a right to freedom as we have." Adams is quoted in Phyllis Lee Levin's *Abigail Adams: A Biography.*

Ashley household. Then one day in 1780, according to an early biography, Mrs. Ashley "in a fit of passion . . . struck at Mum Bett's sister with a heated kitchen shovel. Mum Bett interposed her arm and received the blow, the scar of which she bore to the day of her death."[112] Following this incident, Mum Bett left the Ashleys' home, vowing never to return. She asked a young lawyer named Theodore Sedgwick to help her sue for her freedom in the Massachusetts state courts.

Sedgwick, like many white Patriots in the North, had become increasingly uncomfortable with the idea of slavery during the war, and he promptly agreed to take Mum Bett's case. Yet he was curious as to how an illiterate slave woman had hit upon the idea of suing for her liberty. According to her earliest biographer, Mum Bett replied to Sedgwick's inquiry by declaring "that the 'Bill o' Rights' said that all were born free and equal, and that, as she was not a dumb beast, she was certainly one of the nation."[113] The Bill of Rights Mum Bett referred to was part of the new state constitution of Massachusetts and featured many of the same rights later embodied in the first ten amendments to the U.S. Constitution. Mum Bett explained that she had found out about the Massachusetts Bill of Rights

in the first place by "keepin' still and mindin' things"[114] when she was waiting table on her master and his numerous politician friends.

In 1781 Mum Bett, or Elizabeth Freeman as she was now known, won her case and was set free by court order. Years later, after her death in 1829 at the age of eighty five, Theodore Sedgwick publicly cited Freeman as a prime example of why slavery should be abolished in the United States. Although a slave and a female, Freeman "had nothing of the submissive or subdued character, which succumbs to superior force. . . . Even in her humble station, she had, when occasion required it, an air of command which conferred a degree of dignity. . . . She claimed no distinction; but it was yielded to her from her superior experience, energy, skill, and sagacity [wisdom],"[115] Sedgwick declared.

Two years after Freeman's successful legal fight, slavery was officially declared impermissible in Massachusetts under the state's Bill of Rights. By 1804 all states north of Maryland and Delaware had also emancipated their slaves. In the South, where slavery played a vital part in the economy, however, slavery would remain deeply entrenched for nearly a century following the Revolution.

Elizabeth Freeman courageously insisted that slavery was contrary to the principles of freedom and equality that the Patriots claimed to support. Yet as historians Linda Grant De Pauw and Conover Hunt note, neither Freeman "nor any other woman of her time perceived these principles as promising full equality to the female sex."[116] For a half-century following the Revolutionary War, notwithstanding the vital role members of their sex had taken in attaining American independence, the majority of American women quietly accepted the same constricted legal, economic, and political rights they had endured before the conflict.

Epilogue:
American Women After the Revolutionary War

❦

Despite the contributions women made to the Patriot cause during the Revolutionary War and the political crises that preceded it, the achievement of independence failed to bring a revolution in the rights of American females. For most women, the war's end in 1783 signaled a return to their customary duties within their households and families. As in British America, the property and wages of wives remained strictly under the control of their husbands, and women still could not hold public office, serve in the armed forces, or, with a few exceptions, vote in political elections after the Revolution.

"Remember the Ladies"

Excepting the political writer Thomas Paine, no Patriot spokesman stated or even so much as implied that women were entitled to the same rights they claimed for themselves and other white males. Nor did female Americans of the Revolutionary era demand those rights.

As historian Joan R. Gundersen explains, "Although the war mobilized women politically . . . , the Revolution did not create a feminist consciousness."[117] Apparently, American women were not yet ready to abandon the age-old view of their sex as best suited to a private, domestic role in society rather than a public, political one.

Nonetheless, Patriot ideals of equality and natural rights did inspire individual women to question certain long-held attitudes regarding the treatment of females in their society. For example, in 1776 Abigail Adams wrote a now famous letter to her husband in which she urged John Adams and his fellow congressmen in Philadelphia to "Remember the Ladies,"[118] as they devised a new code of laws for their country. Yet most historians agree that Adams, who repeatedly asserted that women should devote themselves above all to their wifely and motherly duties, was not demanding complete equality for her sex. Instead, she was asking for a modest enlargement of women's legal rights. Specifically, Adams wanted additional legal protection for wives against abusive husbands as well as broader property rights for married women.

Adams's request for more legal rights for married women was all but ignored by her husband and other lawmakers. Women's property rights remained essentially unchanged after 1783, although in some states new laws did make it easier for an unhappily married woman to obtain a divorce. In one state—New Jersey—female property holders (i.e., unmarried women) actually obtained the right to vote in political elections during the war. In 1807, however, that right was repealed by the New Jersey legislature on the grounds that women were more naive and compliant than men and therefore their votes could be manipulated by unscrupulous office seekers.

"Republican Motherhood"

Although women gained little in the way of additional legal and political rights as a consequence of the struggle for independence, the Revolution did bring new importance and dignity to their traditional domestic roles. Most Americans, male and female alike, recognized that women had done a great deal to achieve the Patriot victory. Therefore, it was reasoned that since women had played a vital part in securing American independence, they could and should take a significant role in ensuring the survival of the fledgling American republic as well. That role, both men and women believed, was best played out within the customary female domain of home and hearth.

During the decade following the founding of the American republic, a

Abigail Adams's famous letters to her husband regarding the rights of women were later published in this book.

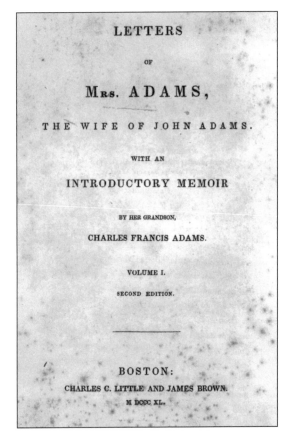

female ideal emerged that has come to be known as "republican motherhood,"[119] a name first coined by historian Linda K. Kerber. According to the concept of republican motherhood, women could crucially influence the success of the infant republic through their role within the family. Their chief duty as republican mothers was to instill in their sons the virtues on which a republican form of government was believed to rest: wisdom, honesty, loyalty, and a compassionate concern for one's fellow citizens. By teaching her sons to understand and cherish these values, a good republican mother helped to ensure that they would grow into virtuous and informed citizens and, if called upon, just and discerning rulers.

In considering how girls and young women could best be readied to fulfill the duties of republican moth-

The most tangible gain for women from the Revolutionary War was the new emphasis on female education.

Women of the American Revolution

erhood, supporters of the concept stressed the importance of education. The leading proponent of female education in the new republic was the writer Judith Sargent Murray, who contended that women had received woefully inadequate schooling in the past. Murray would undoubtedly have agreed with Abigail Adams's assessment of female education in America as "trifling," "narrow," and "contracted."[120] A deeper knowledge of history, philosophy, literature, and world affairs was vital for all females, Murray, Adams, and other backers of educational reform argued, if America's experiment with a republican form of government was to succeed.

Because intellectual training and the responsibilities of republican motherhood were closely linked, probably the most tangible gain for American women from the Revolution was the unprecedented emphasis placed on female education during the postwar era. The Revolutionary War's "most important effect on women," writes historian Rosemarie Zagarri, "was to expand the number, kind, and quality of educational opportunities available to them."[121] In Massachusetts, where the establishment of public elementary schools in every town was made mandatory in 1789, it was stipulated that girls as well as boys be provided with a tax-supported education. And throughout the young republic, private academies sprang up to provide teenage girls from well-off families with the equivalent of a secondary school education.

Although many American women undoubtedly felt a new confidence in their abilities during the postwar era as a result of greater educational opportunities and the respect they were awarded for their role as republican mothers, they did not join together to fight for more rights for their sex. It would not be until the famous Seneca Falls Convention of 1848 that American women would engage in collective protests aimed at expanding their limited political, economic, and legal rights. As the women's rights movement burgeoned in the mid–nineteenth century, women would look back to the Revolutionary era and recall afresh the ideals of equality and liberty proclaimed in the Declaration of Independence. Nearly three-quarters of a century after the declaration was written, American women would finally begin to claim for themselves the legacy of the Revolution that their foremothers had done so much to help achieve.

Notes

Chapter 1: American Women and Prewar Resistance

1. Quoted in Mary Beth Norton, *Liberty's Daughters: The Revolutionary Experience of American Women, 1750–1800*. Boston: Little, Brown, 1980, p. 170.
2. Quoted in Norton, *Liberty's Daughters,* p. 171.
3. Quoted in Norton, *Liberty's Daughters,* p. 170.
4. Quoted in Norton, *Liberty's Daughters,* p. 170.
5. Quoted in Ronald Hoffman and Peter J. Albert, eds., *Women in the Age of the American Revolution.* Charlottesville: University Press of Virginia, 1989, p. 18.
6. Quoted in Joan R. Gundersen, *To Be Useful to the World: Women in Revolutionary America, 1740–1790.* New York: Twayne, 1996, p. 66.
7. Quoted in Carol Berkin, *First Generations: Women in Colonial America.* New York: Hill and Wang, 1996, p. 176.
8. Gundersen, *To Be Useful to the World,* p. 66.
9. Quoted in Norton, *Liberty's Daughters,* p. 169.
10. Quoted in Hoffman and Albert, *Women in the Age of the American Revolution,* p. 227.
11. Quoted in Hoffman and Albert, *Women in the Age of the American Revolution,* pp. 225–26.
12. Quoted in Norton, *Liberty's Daughters,* p. 166.
13. Quoted in Norton, *Liberty's Daughters,* p. 168.
14. Quoted in Linda K. Kerber, *Women of the Republic: Intellect and Ideology in Revolutionary America.* Chapel Hill: University of North Carolina Press, 1980, p. 41.
15. Quoted in Norton, *Liberty's Daughters,* p. 121.
16. Quoted in Rosemarie Zagarri, *A Woman's Dilemma: Mercy Otis Warren and the American Revolution.* Wheeling, IL: Harlan Davidson, 1995, pp. 72–73.

Chapter 2: Patriot Women at War

17. Quoted in Kerber, *Women of the Republic,* p. 104.
18. Quoted in Hoffman and Albert, *Women in the Age of the American Revolution,* p. 33.

19. Quoted in Norton, *Liberty's Daughters,* p. 179.
20. Quoted in Norton, *Liberty's Daughters,* p. 179.
21. Quoted in Kerber, *Women of the Republic,* p. 102.
22. Quoted in Elizabeth F. Ellet, *Revolutionary Women in the War for American Independence: A One-Volume Edition of Elizabeth Ellet's 1848 Landmark Series,* ed. Lincoln Diamant. Westport, CT: Praeger, 1998, p. 99.
23. Quoted in Kerber, *Women of the Republic,* p. 102.
24. Norton, *Liberty's Daughters,* p. 187.
25. Linda Grant De Pauw, *Founding Mothers: Women in America in the Revolutionary Era.* Boston: Houghton Mifflin, 1975, p. 169.
26. Quoted in Cynthia A. Kierner, *Southern Women in Revolution, 1776–1800: Personal and Political Narratives.* Columbia: University of South Carolina Press, 1998, p. 18.
27. Quoted in Linda Grant De Pauw, *Battle Cries and Lullabies: Women in War from Prehistory to the Present.* Norman: University of Oklahoma Press, 1998, p. 124.
28. Quoted in Elizabeth Evans, *Weathering the Storm: Women of the American Revolution.* New York: Charles Scribner's Sons, 1975, pp. 321–22.
29. Quoted in Evans, *Weathering the Storm,* p. 322.
30. Quoted in Evans, *Weathering the Storm,* p. 317.
31. Quoted in Patrick J. Leonard, "As Private Robert Shurtliff, Deborah Samson Served Eighteen Months in the Continental Army," *Military History,* vol. 18, April 2001, p. 24.
32. Quoted in Evans, *Weathering the Storm,* p. 322.
33. Quoted in Evans, *Weathering the Storm,* p. 327.
34. Quoted in Evans, *Weathering the Storm,* p. 328.

Chapter 3: Women Camp Followers

35. Quoted in Holly A. Mayer, *Belonging to the Army: Camp Followers and Community During the American Revolution.* Columbia: University of South Carolina Press, 1996, p. 126.
36. Quoted in Harry M. Ward, *The War for Independence and the Transformation of American Society.* London: UCL, 1999, p. 119.
37. Quoted in Kerber, *Women of the Republic,* p. 57.
38. Quoted in Kerber, *Women of the Republic,* p. 57.
39. Quoted in Mayer, *Belonging to the Army,* p. 131.
40. Quoted in Hoffman and Albert,

Women in the Age of the American Revolution, p. 15.

41. Quoted in Mayer, *Belonging to the Army,* p. 140.

42. Quoted in Ward, *The War for Independence,* p. 118.

43. Quoted in John C. Dann, *The Revolution Remembered: Eyewitness Accounts of the War for Independence.* Chicago: University of Chicago Press, 1980, p. 244.

44. Quoted in Ward, *The War for Independence,* p. 120.

45. Quoted in De Pauw, *Battle Cries and Lullabies,* p. 128.

46. Quoted in Ellet, *Revolutionary Women in the War for American Independence,* p. 120.

47. Quoted in Ellet, *Revolutionary Women in the War for American Independence,* p. 120.

48. Berkin, *First Generations,* p. 188.

Chapter 4: Patriot Women on the Home Front

49. Quoted in Edith B. Gelles, *Portia: The World of Abigail Adams.* Bloomington: Indiana University Press, 1992, p. 41.

50. Quoted in Hoffman and Albert, *Women in the Age of the American Revolution,* p. 230.

51. Quoted in Kierner, *Southern Women in Revolution,* p. 9.

52. Quoted in Norton, *Liberty's Daughters,* p. 204.

53. Quoted in Norton, *Liberty's Daughters,* p. 208.

54. Quoted in Ray Raphael, *A People's History of the American Revolution: How Common People Shaped the Fight for Independence.* New York: New, 2001, p. 132.

55. Quoted in Raphael, *A People's History of the American Revolution,* p. 132.

56. Quoted in Kierner, *Southern Women in Revolution,* p. 18.

57. Gundersen, *To Be Useful to the World,* p. 124.

58. Quoted in Berkin, *First Generations,* p. 164.

59. Quoted in Evans, *Weathering the Storm,* p. 26.

60. Quoted in Norton, *Liberty's Daughters,* pp. 202–203.

61. Quoted in Evans, *Weathering the Storm,* pp. 26–27.

62. Quoted in Ward, *The War for Independence,* p. 150.

63. Norton, *Liberty's Daughters,* p. 216.

64. Quoted in Norton, *Liberty's Daughters,* pp. 216–17.

65. Quoted in Norton, *Liberty's Daughters,* p. 215.

66. Berkin, *First Generations,* p. 182.

67. Joy Day Buel and Richard Buel, *The Way of Duty: A Woman and Her*

Family in Revolutionary America. New York: W. W. Norton, 1984, p. 116.

68. Quoted in Phyllis Lee Levin, *Abigail Adams: A Biography.* New York: Ballantine Books, 1987, p. 36.

69. Quoted in Gelles, *Portia,* p. 38.

70. Quoted in Gelles, *Portia,* pp. 39–40.

71. Quoted in Gelles, *Portia,* p. 40.

Chapter 5: Loyalist and Pacifist Women

72. Janice Potter-MacKinnon, *While the Women Wept: Loyalist Refugee Women in Eastern Ontario.* Montreal: McGill-Queen's University Press, 1993, p. 70.

73. Quoted in Potter-Mackinnon, *While the Women Wept,* p. 52.

74. Quoted in Potter-MacKinnon, *While the Women Wept,* p. 54.

75. Quoted in Potter-MacKinnon, *While the Women Wept,* p. 54.

76. Quoted in Evans, *Weathering the Storm,* p. 191.

77. Quoted in Evans, *Weathering the Storm,* pp. 238–39.

78. Quoted in Norton, *Liberty's Daughters,* p. 174.

79. Quoted in De Pauw, *Founding Mothers,* p. 129.

80. Quoted in Norton, *Liberty's Daughters,* pp. 175–76.

81. Quoted in De Pauw, *Founding Mothers,* p. 138.

82. Quoted in Raphael, *A People's History of the American Revolution,* p. 181.

83. Quoted in Norton, *Liberty's Daughters,* p. 218.

84. Quoted in Evans, *Weathering the Storm,* pp. 294–95.

Chapter 6: Native American Women

85. Barbara Graymount, *The Iroquois in the American Revolution.* Syracuse, NY: Syracuse University Press, 1972, p. 1.

86. Potter-MacKinnon, *While the Women Wept,* p. 18.

87. Quoted in De Pauw, *Founding Mothers,* p. 123.

88. Gundersen, *To Be Useful to the World,* p. 157.

89. Quoted in Potter-MacKinnon, *While the Women Wept,* p. 56.

90. Quoted in De Pauw, *Founding Mothers,* p. 122.

91. Quoted in James E. Seaver, ed., *A Narrative of the Life of Mary Jemison.* Norman: University of Oklahoma Press, 1992, p. 100.

92. Quoted in Seaver, *A Narrative of the Life of Mary Jemison,* pp. 104–105.

93. Quoted in Seaver, *A Narrative of the*

Life of Mary Jemison, pp. 102–103.

94. Quoted in Raphael, *A People's History of the American Revolution,* p. 226.

95. Quoted in Raphael, *A People's History of the American Revolution,* p. 223.

96. De Pauw, *Founding Mothers,* p. 123.

Chapter 7: African American Women

97. Quoted in Hoffman and Albert, *Women in the Age of the American Revolution,* p. 325.

98. Quoted in Sylvia R. Frey, *Water from the Rock: Black Resistance in a Revolutionary Age.* Princeton, NJ: Princeton University Press, 1991, p. 117.

99. Frey, *Water from the Rock,* p. 134.

100. Quoted in Ward, *The War for Independence,* p. 46.

101. Quoted in Jeffrey J. Crowe and Larry E. Tise, eds., *The Southern Experience in the American Revolution.* Chapel Hill: University of North Carolina Press, 1978, p. 213.

102. Quoted in Raphael, *A People's History of the American Revolution,* p. 262.

103. Quoted in Hoffman and Albert, *Women in the Age of the American Revolution,* p. 328.

104. Raphael, *A People's History of the American Revolution,* p. 262.

105. Frey, *Water from the Rock,* p. 127.

106. Quoted in Raphael, *A People's History of the American Revolution,* p. 259.

107. Quoted in Sidney Kaplan and Emma Nogrady Kaplan, *The Black Presence in the Era of the American Revolution.* Amherst: University of Massachusetts Press, 1989, p. 171.

108. Quoted in Kaplan and Kaplan, *The Black Presence in the Era of the American Revolution,* p. 174.

109. Quoted in Kaplan and Kaplan, *The Black Presence in the Era of the American Revolution,* p. 182.

110. Quoted in Kaplan and Kaplan, *The Black Presence in the Era of the American Revolution,* p. 186.

111. Quoted in Merle Richmond, *Phillis Wheatley.* New York: Chelsea House, 1988, pp. 169–70.

112. Quoted in Kaplan and Kaplan, *The Black Presence in the Era of the American Revolution,* p. 244.

113. Quoted in Kaplan and Kaplan, *The Black Presence in the Era of the American Revolution,* p. 245.

114. Quoted in Kaplan and Kaplan,

The Black Presence in the Era of the American Revolution, p. 245.

115. Quoted in Kaplan and Kaplan, *The Black Presence in the Era of the American Revolution*, p. 246.

116. Linda Grant De Pauw and Conover Hunt, *Remember the Ladies: Women in America, 1750–1815*. New York: Viking, 1976, p. 153.

Epilogue: American Women After the Revolutionary War

117. Gundersen, *To Be Useful to the World*, p. 167.

118. Quoted in Levin, *Abigail Adams*, p. 82.

119. Kerber, *Women of the Republic*, p. 11.

120. Quoted in Norton, *Liberty's Daughters*, p. 262.

121. Zagarri, *A Woman's Dilemma*, p. 178.

For Further Reading

Natalie S. Bober, *Abigail Adams: Witness to Revolution.* New York: Atheneum Books, 1995. A carefully researched account of one of the best-known women of the Revolutionary era.

Drollene P. Brown, *Sybil Rides for Independence.* Niles, IL: Albert Whitman, 1985. A brief account of the nighttime ride of Sybil Ludington, who has been called the female Paul Revere.

Patricia Edwards Clyne, *Patriots in Petticoats.* New York: Dodd, Mead, 1976. This book includes short biographies of fifteen women who played important roles in the Revolutionary War.

Mary R. Furbee, *Wild Rose: Nancy Ward and the Cherokee Nation.* Greensboro, NC: Morgan Reynolds, 2001. A good recent biography of the Cherokee leader.

——, *Women of the American Revolution.* San Diego: Lucent Books, 1999. Includes biographies of six leading women of the Revolutionary era, including Deborah Samson, Abigail Adams, and Mercy Otis Warren.

Merle Richmond, *Phillis Wheatley.* New York: Chelsea House, 1988. An informative biography of America's first African American female poet.

Mary Wilds, *Mumbet: The Life and Times of Elizabeth Freeman: The True Story of a Slave Who Won Her Freedom.* Greensboro, NC: Avisson, 1999. A biography of the African American slave Elizabeth Freeman, who successfully sued for her freedom in the Massachusetts courts during the Revolution.

P. M. Zall, *Becoming American: Young People in the American Revolution.* Hamden, CT: Linnet Books, 1993. This history provides fascinating excerpts from diaries, letters, and other primary sources written by young women and men who lived through the Revolutionary War.

Karen Zeinert, *Those Remarkable Women of the American Revolution.* Brookfield, CT: Millbrook, 1996. This book describes the various roles that women played during the Revolution.

Works Consulted

Books

Carol Berkin, *First Generations: Women in Colonial America.* New York: Hill and Wang, 1996. This book includes a chapter on the impact of the Revolutionary War on women.

Phyllis R. Blakeley, ed., *Eleven Exiles: Accounts of Loyalists of the American Revolution.* Toronto: Dundurn, 1982. This history includes a chapter on the Mohawk Loyalist leader Molly Brant.

Joy Day Buel and Richard Buel, *The Way of Duty: A Woman and Her Family in Revolutionary America.* New York: W. W. Norton, 1984. This biography of Mary Silliman, a Connecticut woman whose husband served on the Patriot side, reveals how disruptive the Revolutionary War was to the everyday lives of women and their families.

Colin G. Calloway, *The American Revolution in Indian Country: Crisis and Diversity in Native American Communities.* Cambridge, UK: Cambridge University Press, 1995. A detailed account of how the war affected and was affected by Native Americans.

Charles E. Claghorn, *Women Patriots of the American Revolution: A Biographical Dictionary.* Metuchen, NJ: Scarecrow, 1991. This book includes biographical sketches of more than five hundred women.

Jeffrey J. Crowe and Larry E. Tise, eds., *The Southern Experience in the American Revolution.* Chapel Hill: University of North Carolina Press, 1978. This history includes an essay by Mary Beth Norton on the impact of the American Revolution on southern women.

John C. Dann, *The Revolution Remembered: Eyewitness Accounts of the War for Independence.* Chicago: University of Chicago Press, 1980. This collection of primary sources includes an autobiographical sketch by Sarah Osborn, a camp follower with the Continental Army.

Linda Grant De Pauw, *Battle Cries and Lullabies: Women in War from Prehistory to the Present.* Norman: University of Oklahoma Press, 1998. This history includes a section on American women in the

Revolutionary War.

———— *Founding Mothers: Women in America in the Revolutionary Era.* Boston: Houghton Mifflin, 1975. De Pauw offers a detailed account of women's everyday lives during the Revolutionary era.

Linda Grant De Pauw and Conover Hunt, *Remember the Ladies: Women in America, 1750–1815.* New York: Viking, 1976. Suitable for older students, this richly illustrated volume includes an interesting chapter on women and the Revolution.

Elizabeth F. Ellet, *Revolutionary Women in the War for American Independence: A One-Volume Revised Edition of Elizabeth Ellet's 1848 Landmark Series.* Ed. Lincoln Diamant. Westport, CT: Praeger, 1998. This classic work includes biographies of more than eighty women who played significant roles in the Revolution.

Elizabeth Evans, *Weathering the Storm: Women of the American Revolution.* New York: Charles Scribner's Sons, 1975. This is a collection of excerpts from the diaries, letters, and other writings of eleven American women who lived through the Revolution.

Sylvia R. Frey, *Water from the Rock: Black Resistance in a Revolutionary Age.* Princeton, NJ: Princeton University Press, 1991. This text details the experiences of African American slaves during the Revolutionary era.

Edith B. Gelles, *Portia: The World of Abigail Adams.* Bloomington: Indiana University Press, 1992. A scholarly account of Abigail Adams and her times.

Barbara Graymount, *The Iroquois in the American Revolution.* Syracuse, NY: Syracuse University Press, 1972. This history includes information on the influential Mohawk leader Molly Brant.

Joan R. Gundersen, *To Be Useful to the World: Women in Revolutionary America, 1740–1790.* New York: Twayne, 1996. This book examines the wartime experiences of American women from all social, racial, and economic groups.

Ronald Hoffman and Peter J. Albert, eds., *Women in the Age of the American Revolution.* Charlottesville: University Press of Virginia, 1989. A collection of essays on different aspects of women's experiences in the Revolutionary era by leading scholars in the field of women's history.

Sidney Kaplan and Emma Nogrady Kaplan, *The Black Presence in the Era of the American Revolution.* Amherst: University of Massachusetts Press,

1989. This book includes useful sections on Phillis Wheatley and Elizabeth Freeman.

Linda K. Kerber, *Women of the Republic: Intellect and Ideology in Revolutionary America*. Chapel Hill: University of North Carolina Press, 1980. A detailed account of women's political roles during the Revolutionary era.

Cynthia A. Kierner, *Southern Women in Revolution, 1776–1800: Personal and Political Narratives*. Columbia: University of South Carolina Press, 1998. This history examines the wartime experiences of southern women of various social and economic classes.

Phyllis Lee Levin, *Abigail Adams: A Biography*. New York: Ballantine Books, 1987. A comprehensive biography of one of the Revolutionary era's most famous women.

Holly A. Mayer, *Belonging to the Army: Camp Followers and Community During the American Revolution*. Columbia: University of South Carolina Press, 1996. A detailed study of camp followers in the Continental Army.

Mary Beth Norton, *Liberty's Daughters: The Revolutionary Experience of American Women, 1750–1800*. Boston: Little, Brown, 1980. One of the most comprehensive and respected accounts of women's experiences during the Revolutionary era.

Janice Potter-MacKinnon, *While the Women Wept: Loyalist Refugee Women in Eastern Ontario*. Montreal: McGill-Queen's University Press, 1993. This book traces the experiences of Loyalist women living in the Northeast during the Revolutionary War.

Ray Raphael, *A People's History of the American Revolution: How Common People Shaped the Fight for Independence*. New York: New, 2001. This history tells the story of the Revolution from the viewpoint of ordinary Americans, including poor women, Native American women, and slave women.

Marylynn Salmon, *The Limits of Independence: American Women, 1760–1800. Young Oxford History of Women in the United States*. Vol. 3. New York: Oxford University Press, 1997. An account of women's lives and contributions during and after the Revolutionary era by a leading scholar of women's history.

James E. Seaver, ed., *A Narrative of the Life of Mary Jemison*. Norman: University of Oklahoma Press, 1992. Originally published in 1824, Mary Jemison's autobiography details her life as a white Seneca before, during, and after the Revolutionary War.

Harry M. Ward, *The War for Independence and the Transformation of American Society.* London: UCL, 1999. This book includes chapters on women on the home front and women camp followers.

Betty Wood, "The Impact of the Revolution on the Role, Status, and Experience of Women," in *The Blackwell Encyclopedia of the American Revolution.* Ed. Jack P. Greene and J. R. Pole. Cambridge, MA: Blackwell Reference, 1991. A brief but useful essay on the consequences of the Revolutionary War for American women.

Rosemarie Zagarri, *A Woman's Dilemma: Mercy Otis Warren and the American Revolution.* Wheeling, IL: Harlan Davidson, 1995. A scholarly biography of the Revolutionary War's most famous female propagandist.

Periodical

Patrick J. Leonard, "As Private Robert Shurtliff, Deborah Samson Served Eighteen Months in the Continental Army," *Military History* vol. 18, April 2001. An account of the best-known female soldier of the Revolutionary War.

Internet Sources

Susan M. Bazely, "Who Was Molly Brant?" Cataraqui Archaeological Research Foundation, 1996. http://web.ctsolutions.com. This site includes a detailed biography of Brant and a useful discussion of her role in the Revolutionary War.

Gale Group Free Resources: Women's History Month, Biographies, "Nancy Ward: Cherokee Tribal Leader," 2001. www.gale.com. A short but helpful biography of the Cherokee leader.

Index

Abigail Adams: A Biography (Levin), 62
Adams, Abigail, 55, 62, 65–67, 103
Adams, John, 25, 55, 65
Adulateur, The (Mercy Otis Warren), 25
African American women
  attempts to gain freedom by, 96–100
  effects of wartime shortages on, 94–96
  first published poet among, 100–102
  roles of, 93–94
Albert, Peter J., 58
Amish, 77
Andre, John, 74
Arnold, Benedict, 74
Arnold, Peggy Shippen, 74
Ashley, John, 103–104
Association, the 28–31

Bailey, Anne Trotter, 37
Bartton, Martha, 35
Bates, Ann, 73–74
*Battle Cries and Lullabies: Women in War from Prehistory
  to the Present* (De Pauw), 50
Battle of Monmouth, 52
Battle of Oriskany, 85–86, 88
Battle of Saratoga, 10
Battle of Yorktown, 38, 44
Beloved Woman, 89–91
Berkin, Carol, 54, 64–65
Bett, Mum. See Freeman, Elizabeth
*Black Presence in the Era of the American Revolution,
  The* (Kaplan and Kaplan), 101
black women. *See* African American women
bleeding, 48
Blue Ridge Mountains, 92
Bonnie Prince Charlie, 75
Boston, Massachusetts, 19, 39–40, 62
Boston Evening Post (newspaper), 21
Boston Tea Party, 9
Boudinot, Susan, 19

Braintree, Massachusetts, 65
Brant, Molly, 83–86
Bridgewater, Connecticut, 20–21
British
  camp followers of, 44
  defeated by Americans, 10
  plundering by, 59
  soldiers rape American women, 61–63
  treatment of escaped slaves by, 96–100
Brookfield, New Hampshire, 20
Buel, Joy Day, 65
Buel, Richard, 65
Burgin, Elizabeth, 32

camp followers
  as nurses, 46–48
  tasks performed by, 45–46
  Washington's dislike of, 41–45
  as water carriers, 50
Canada, 76–77, 87
Cape Fear River, 76
Caribbean, 76
Carolina, 90
Cayuga, 85
Cherokee, 89–92
Chota, 92
Clarke, Charity, 15
Clinton, Henry, 96
Concord, Massachusetts, 10, 35
confiscation, 58–61
Congress, 9–10, 59
Connecticut, 20–21, 31–32, 61
Connecticut Farms, 63
Continental army
  Darragh stops surprise attack on camp of, 33
  Frazier delivers supplies to, 29
  number of African Americans who served in,
    100
  organization of, 10

see also camp followers
Continental Congress, 70, 85
Cooke, Florence, 71
Corbin, John, 50
Corbin, Margaret Cochrin, 49–54
cornstalks, 58
Council of Chiefs, 89
coverture, 70
Cummings, Anne, 24
Cummings, Betsy, 24

Danbury, Connecticut, 31–32
Darragh, Lydia, 33
Daughters of Liberty, 19–20, 56–57
Declaration of Independence, 10, 103
Defeat, The (Mercy Otis Warren), 25
Delaware, 31
de Luzerne, Countess, 30
demonstrations, 21
De Pauw, Linda Grant, 31, 50, 73, 92, 105
Diamant, Lincoln, 52
Dibblee, Filer, 76–77
Dibblee, Polly, 76–77
Dunmore, Lord, 96, 98
dysentery, 48

Edenton Petition, 22–24
Evans, Elizabeth, 95
exile, 76–79

Fergusson, Elizabeth Graeme, 73
Fergusson, Hugh, 73
First Generations: Women in Colonial America
    (Berkin), 64
Fisher, Sally, 78
Fisher, Thomas, 78–79
Five Civilized Tribes, 89
Fort Edward, 88
Fort Henry, 91
Fort Niagara, 84–86
Fort Stanwix, 85
Fort Washington, 50
Franklin, Benjamin, 15
Franklin, Sarah, 15
Frazier, Mary, 29
Freeman, Elizabeth, 102–105

Frey, Sylvia R., 96, 98
fund-raisers, 27–31
funeral processions, 21

Gadsden, Christopher, 17
Galloway, Grace Growden, 71–72
Galloway, Joseph, 71
Gannett, Benjamin, 38
Gay, Sam. *See* Bailey, Anne Trotter
Geiger, Emily, 32–33
Genessee River, 88
Ghighua (Beloved Woman), 89
Graymount, Barbara, 83–84
Great Britain, 76
Greene, Nathanael, 32–33
Groton, Massachusetts, 35
Group, The (Mercy Otis Warren), 25
Gundersen, Joan R., 19, 61, 85

hangings, 21
Hart, Nancy Morgan, 36
Hays, Mary Ludwig, 49–54
Henry, Elizabeth, 73
Hessians, 59, 61, 63
"History Can Do It No Justice: Women and the
    Reinterpretation of the American Revolution"
    (Kerber), 58
Hoffman, Ronald, 58
Holmes, Lorenda, 74–75
Hooper, Anne, 15
Hunt, Conover, 105

inflation, 55–58
Intolerable Acts, 9
Iroquois, 82–89
Iroquois in the American Revolution, The (Graymount),
    84
Itch, the, 49

Jackson, Andrew, 92
Jefferson, Thomas, 96
Jemison, Mary, 87–89
Jewett Bridge, 35
Johnson, Mary, 49
Johnson, William, 84–85
Jones, Jacqueline, 94, 97

Joseph, 85, 87

Kaplan, Emma Nogrady, 101
Kaplan, Sidney, 101
Kerber, Linda K., 17, 29, 45, 58, 71
Konwatsi'tsiaienni. *See* Brant, Molly

Langston, Laodicea "Dicey," 34–35
Lee, Ann, 77
Levin, Phyllis Lee, 62
Lexington, Massachusetts, 10, 35
liberty teas, 17–18
Liberty's Daughters: The Revolutionary Experience of American Women (Mary Beth Norton), 24
Lindsey, Abigail, 70–71
Lindsey, John, 71
Little Beard, 89
London, 102
Loyalists
    become exiles, 76–77
    differences between Patriot families and, 68–69
    Patriots seize property of, 70–71
    persecution of, 68–71
    population of, 10
    women's support of, 24, 73–76, 83–85
Ludington, Sybil, 31–32

MacDonald, Allan, 75–76
MacDonald, Flora, 75–76
maple syrup, 58
Martin, Joseph Plumb, 42, 52–53
Maryland, 31
Massachusetts
    Abigail Adams takes charge of family farm in, 65–67
    British fight colonists in, 9–10
    Freeman sues for her freedom from slavery in, 104
    Groton women guard Jewett Bridge in, 35
    Revere's ride through, 31
    women recall terror of fighting in, 64
Massachusetts Bill of Rights, 104
McCrea, Jane, 88
Mennonites, 77
messengers, 31–33
Mississippi River, 92

Mohawk, 83–85
molasses, 58
Moravians, 77
Morris, Mary, 29
Mother Ann. *See* Lee, Ann
Motte, Rebecca, 35

Nagle, Jacob, 45
Nanye'hi. *See* Ward, Nancy
Native American women
    roles of, 81–83
    support of Loyalists by, 83–86
    support of Patriots by, 87, 89–92
Negro women. See African American women
New England, 77
New Hampshire Gazette (newspaper), 19
New Jersey, 31, 52, 61–63, 103
New York
    Americans defeat British in, 10
    Iroquois raid American settlements in, 85
    McCrea ambushed by Iroquois in, 88
    Patriots loot Brant's estate in, 86
    prison ships in, 32
    rapes in, 61–62
    Shakers founded in, 77
    women saboteurs in, 35
New York City, 32, 61, 76
North Carolina, 76, 92
Norton, Azubah, 64
Norton, Mary Beth, 24, 31, 63, 82
Nova Scotia, 99–100
nurses, 46–48

Oneida, 87, 89
Osborn, Sarah, 49
Otis, James, 24

pacifists, 77–80
Parliament, 8–9
Patriots
    differences between Loyalist families and, 68–69
    loot Brant's estate, 86
    protest British taxes, 9–10
    recruit women for political activities, 16–22
    seize Loyalists' property, 70–71
    support freedom of slaves, 103

women's support of
    by African Americans, 95, 100–102
    as fund-raisers, 27–31
    as messengers, 31–33
    by Native Americans, 87, 89–92
    as saboteurs, 35
    as soldiers, 36–40
    as spies, 33–35
Penn, William, 78
Pennsylvania, 33, 78, 103
Pennsylvania Evening Post (newspaper), 58
Pennsylvania Executive Council, 50
Pennsylvania Magazine, 102
Peters, John, 102
Philadelphia, Pennsylvania, 71–72, 79–80
Phyllis, 30
pins, 58
Pitcher, Molly. *See* Hays, Mary Ludwig
pleurisy, 48
plunder, 58–61
pneumonia, 48
Potter-MacKinnon, Janice, 68, 84
prison ships, 32
Proclamation of 1763, 83
putrid fever, 48

Quakers, 77–80, 103

rape, 61–63
Raphael, Ray, 97
Rawdon, Lord, 61
Rawle, Anne, 79–80
Redcoats, 10
Reed, Esther de Berdt, 27–31, 50
Reed, Joseph, 50
Revere, Paul, 31, 38
robbers, 59

saboteurs, 35
salt, 57–58
Samson, Deborah, 37–40
Saratoga, New York, 35
scarcity of goods, 55–58
Schuyler, Catherine, 35
Sedgwick, Theodore, 104
Seider, Christopher, 101

Seneca, 85, 87–88
Sentiments of an American Woman (Esther de Berdt
    Reed), 27
Shakers, 77
Shattuck, Sarah, 35
Shawnee, 91
Shurtliff, Robert. See Samson, Deborah
Sillman, Mary Fish, 65
slaves
    attempts to gain freedom by, 96–100, 102–105
    effects of wartime shortages on, 94–96
    first published poet among, 100–102
    roles of, 93–94
smallpox, 48
Society of Friends. See Quakers
soldiers, 36–40
Sons of Liberty, 19
South Carolina, 35, 60
South Carolina Gazette (newspaper), 20
spies, 33–35
spinning, 18–22
Stamp Act, 8–9
Staten Island, New York, 61
St. Clair, Sally, 37
sugar, 58
Sullivan, John, 85, 88
Sumter, Thomas, 32
syrup, 58

tarring and featherings, 21
tea boycott, 17–19
Tennessee, 91–92
thorns, 58
thread, 58
Tories. *See* Loyalists
Townshend duties, 9
Treaty of Paris, 10
tuberculosis, 48
Tuscarora, 87
typhoid, 48

U.S. Constitution, 104

Valley Forge, Pennsylvania, 29, 48, 79
Virginia, 31, 90, 92
vomiting, 48

walnut ashes, 58

War for Independence and the Transformation of American Society, The (Harry Ward), 44

Ward, Bryant, 90

Ward, Harry, 44

Ward, Nancy, 89–92

Warren, James, 24, 66

Warren, Mercy Otis, 24–26

Washington, George

confronts Peggy Shippen Arnold, 74

dislikes camp followers, 41–45

Quaker women petition to return husbands from exile, 78–79

refuses cash gifts for soldiers, 30–31

slaves escape from estate of, 96

Wheatley's poem in honor of, 101–102

Washington, Martha, 48

Watauga River, 91

water carriers, 50

Weathering the Storm: Women of the American Revolution (Evans), 95

weavers, 19

Wells, Rachel, 59

West Point, New York, 38, 51–52

West Virginia, 91

Wheatley, John, 100, 102

Wheatley, Phillis, 100–102

Wheatley, Susannah, 100

white plague, 48

Whitemarsh, Pennsylvania, 33

Wilkinson, Eliza, 60–61

Winslow, Anna, 19

Winthrop, Hannah, 44, 64

women

political activities of, 16–24

problems faced by, during American Revolution

confiscation and plunder, 58–61

inflation and scarcity, 55–58

rape, 61–63

roles of

changes in, 63–65

as fund-raisers, 27–31

as messengers, 31–33

as nurses, 46–48

as pacifists, 77–80

before the Revolutionary War, 10–13, 81–83, 93–94

as saboteurs, 35

as soldiers, 36–40

as spies, 33–35

as water carriers, 50

see also African American women; Native American women

Women in the Age of the American Revolution (Hoffman and Albert), 58

Women of the Republic (Kerber), 17, 29, 71

Wright, Prudence, 35

yarn, 58

Zane, Elizabeth, 91

Picture Credits

❦

Cover Photo: © Owen Franken/
   CORBIS
© Bettmann/CORBIS, 12, 23, 79, 86,
   108
© CORBIS, 15
© Hulton Archive, 11, 16, 28, 30, 34,
   36, 39, 42, 43, 47, 56, 66, 69, 75, 78,
   82, 90, 94, 97, 99, 100, 107

© Hulton-Deutsch Collection/
   CORBIS, 60
© Catherine Karnow/CORBIS, 18,
   51
Library of Congress, 53
© Richard T. Nowitz/CORBIS, 46
© G.E. Kidder Smith/CORBIS, 22,
   57

About the Author

Louise Chipley Slavicek received her master's degree in American history from the University of Connecticut. She has written many articles on historical subjects and is the author of two other books for Lucent Books, *Life Among the Puritans* and *Confucianism*. She lives in Ohio with her husband, Jim, a research biologist, and her children, Krista and Nathan.